ROVE EXPOSED

ROVE EXPOSED

HOW
BUSH'S BRAIN
FOOLED AMERICA

JAMES MOORE AND **WAYNE SLATER**

WILEY

John Wiley & Sons, Inc.

Contents

FOREWORD   VII

INTRODUCTION: KING KARL OR MR. CO-PRESIDENT?   1

1   OFF TO THE SHOW   9

2   CONSULTANT, BUG THYSELF   17

3   POLITICALLY PARANORMAL   27

4   LIVIN' WITH THE LONG KNIVES   39

5   RUNNING FOR COVER   51

6   PROOF OF PERFORMANCE   63

7   THE BOY WHO FORGOT TO BE A BOY   69

8   GONE TO TEXAS   91

9   REFINING THE CRUDE   103

10   TO THE VICTOR   115

11   CONTESTS WITHOUT RULES   125

12   PRODUCT LAUNCH   141

13 EVERYTHING MATTERS   151

14 WHOSE DREAM IS THIS, ANYWAY?   165

15 ROVIAN CANCER   177

NOTES   197

INDEX   217

ABOUT THE AUTHORS   225

Foreword

The authors have been arguing (we hope forcefully) for many years that Karl Rove was going to displace traditional thinking about politics and government. We think the evidence, which is everything Karl has done since he began to work on a national stage, proves this point. The politically obsessed kid from Salt Lake City, Utah, has lived and worked with such single-mindedness that he has overcome a number of events that might have been ruinous for his president. Instead, Rove has grown skilled at changing the subject matter, denying the facts, calling people unpatriotic, and helping President Bush conduct his job as if there were not a storm raging outside his door.

In the aftermath of Hurricane Katrina, Karl Rove's influence was readily understandable and visible in the federal government's disaster response. Rove has cultivated a political philosophy that turns the government and its agencies into a vehicle for delivering votes and influence and not services to the people who pay taxes. Money only goes to favorite causes of the president and his supporters. Federal bureaucracies are reduced in size until they are rendered near meaningless. Jobs running important agencies are given to people who have proven to be significant fund-raisers for the president or are long-time political associates. This goes beyond mere patronage or cronyism. Appointments are by a design that guarantees leadership will do little or nothing and spend virtually nothing. When the time came for the government to respond after Katrina devastated

New Orleans, there simply was not much of a government to act and what little there was lacked guidance.

The vindictiveness Rove used throughout his political career in Texas has also been manifest in the national arena throughout both Bush campaigns and terms in office. As long-time observers of Rove (dating back to 1979), we believe suspicions of his involvement in the leaking of an undercover agent's name to be well placed. Rove is also not beyond lying about his role in any leak. At a minimum, he will parse his own language to accomplish what one of his heroes once referred to as a "nondenial denial." He is good at this. Because Rove has been without fear every time he has ever been confronted for his deceits, he may have stumbled and lied to the grand jury or federal investigators looking into the case of CIA agent Valerie Plame. Rove reportedly told the grand jury and the FBI that he did not speak to anyone about the agent or provide her name until he read it in a syndicated column by Robert Novak. Both the e-mails and the testimony of *Time* magazine reporter Matt Cooper proved both of those claims to be false. Lies of this nature can lead to charges of perjury or obstruction of justice and prosecutor Patrick Fitzgerald, who is heading up the case, has a reputation of taking it personally when he is lied to.

We have seen nothing in Karl Rove's behavior that has surprised us. His attempt to reform social security is part of a larger plan to destroy a federal program that Democrats are given political credit for. His counsel to the president on Israel and the Mideast has little to do with what is best for the region and the people hoping for peace. Rove affects a completely pro-Israel stance because he has been hoping for many years to steer dollars of Jewish donors away from the Democrats and into the pockets of Republicans. And it has been working.

Karl Rove understands marketing and branding and messages and positioning to a degree that is without precedent in U.S. political history. Creating policy and accomplishing goals is not what counts. Creating power and winning elections is all that matters. And he does that by using the government, all of its institutions, the people who have power and money, to set up the next electoral victory. Government becomes a part of his massive machine.

His greatest talent, however, may be his ability to understand and manipulate the electoral process by crunching statistics, pushing money into the system, and finding issues and messages to tear people apart and negatively motivate them to go vote. Rove carries details in his head many local precinct workers do not know and he uses them to help him win. And if ever there are problems, he easily changes the discussion to a new one, which he and his candidate can control.

Katrina is only the most recent example of this skill. As the federal government managed by George W. Bush failed to adequately respond to the national disaster, the federal government began talking about the mayor of New Orleans and the governor and how the state and local governments ought to have acted sooner to ask for federal help. Both the mayor and the governor were Democrats so it was politically easy for Rove to push the blame downward, even though only the federal government has the resources to respond to such national disasters. The goal is always to protect the president who, in this particular case, appeared lost and bumbling to a degree never before seen.

Karl Rove has taken his place in history. His profile has found purchase in the unseemly and the untrue. But it has also produced a record of great achievement. He wins. Constantly, Karl Rove wins. He finds the money and the candidates and the issues and then he works harder and smarter than anyone ever has. He does whatever it takes to achieve victory and that means that he will push up to the edge of the law to harm and conquer. All of this says Rove is the best. It says he knows what he is doing in a way no other political and policy expert has ever known. It says Karl Rove understands how to raise money and how to use it to influence our electoral processes.

But what does it say about our democracy. What does the rise of Karl Rove say about us?

JAMES C. MOORE

Austin, Texas
September 2005

"Power is not alluring to pure minds."

Thomas Jefferson

Introduction:
King Karl or Mr. Co-President?

The measure of the man is what he does with power.
—Pittacus

There are still people in America who do not know about Karl Rove. But everyone in the United States has been affected by Rove's influence in the White House. Karl Rove, master political strategist and policy adviser to President George W. Bush, matters to all Americans, many who have never even heard his name. While the president chafes at the description of Rove as, "Bush's Brain," he can hardly deny that every policy and political decision either goes through, or comes from, the consultant. In political circles, there is frequent discussion, almost as a parlor game, of where Karl Rove ends and George Bush begins. The relationship between the president and Rove has transcended all of the traditional models.

"I think he's more in a position of grooming the president than in being a subordinate to the president, as I perceive it. It's pretty unusual," University of Texas political scientist Bruce Buchanan claimed.

Rove is shaping policy based on politics. He reads the polls and studies political trends and then argues for policies that point in the same direction. Asked to confirm the premise, Rove quickly turned the proposition on its head: politics is an instrument for accomplishing the president's policies, not the other way around.

"The politics at the White House is less about how does this impact us politically and more about how do you go about politically, go out here and make the case for this and who do you make the case to?"

Regardless, *Time* magazine's White House correspondent, James Carney, said, "Karl Rove is probably the most influential and important political consultant to a president that we've ever seen."

The relationship between the president and his guru ought to be, at a minimum, subject to intense scrutiny. Normally, the campaign consultant maintains a professional detachment as a hired hand, someone who is able, unlike the candidate's volunteers and supporters, to step forward with unvarnished honesty. In Rove's case, there is no such professional separation between him and his client. Bush and his consultant are friends, peers, trusted confidantes, and admirers of each other. The relationship is, almost by definition, co-dependent. Neither man is able to operate independently and remain whole in his political endeavors. And the president has elevated Rove to unprecedented power in his second term. Karl Rove's portfolio has come to include domestic and foreign policy along with political strategies. The most critical dynamics of their relationship have not changed, though.

Bush is the product. And Rove is the marketer. One cannot succeed without the other.

The president's critics often overstate the case in efforts to discredit Bush. He is neither as intellectual as his circle of advisors want the world to believe nor is he as dim as portrayed by Democrats. Opponents have frequently underestimated Bush's ability to build coalitions and win the day for his arguments. But Rove was the whetstone that sharpened Bush into a presidential device. In both presidential campaigns and in the White House, Rove's choices became the president's policies.

The inherent danger in an arrangement where the political advisor also drives policy is that the consultant is deciding what is best for the next election cycle and his political party while the president needs to be considering what best serves the country beyond Election Day. These two interests are frequently divergent and in conflict. While the president does have considerable personal and political strengths, Rove has carried into their collaborations a rigorous intellect, superior political expertise, and capacity for detail.

The end result is obvious: Karl Rove thinks it, and George W. Bush does it.

That's the way it works. And it works well. Rove's political strategies are steering administration decisions on domestic issues and foreign policy. Karl Rove's political calculations have proved more often right than wrong and, for a president interested in reelection, a formula that sways a constituency or adds electoral votes is something he cannot afford to ignore. Rove's increase of the conservative evangelical base in the 2004 reelection campaign serves as substantive proof that he is both instinctive and scientific in a manner that has exceeded previous successful strategists.

Karl Rove has turned his role into something grander than just presidential political advisor, though. While he has several White House titles, Rove is largely responsible for the politics that got George W. Bush elected, and remains instrumental in the policies that have resulted. His influence marks a transcendent moment in American politics: the rise of an unelected consultant to a position of unprecedented power. Secretary of State Colin Powell, for example, had influence over policy, but not a close, long-standing relationship with the president. And Bush's pal from Midland, Texas, Secretary of Commerce Don Evans has the friendship, but not the wide-ranging influence over policy while serving in the administration.

Rove has both.

The influence of Karl Rove on the president may raise constitutional questions. But there is little doubt about the practical implications of his position. Rove has a more profound influence on American lives than most officeholders.

He is the co-president of the United States.

And Americans cannot deny his influence.

Rove's policy choices for the president are almost certain to have impact on individual consumers. If, for instance, the price of automobiles began to increase because of the cost of raw materials, Karl Rove's politics may be assigned the blame. The value of some types of steel rose because of a strategic political move by Rove. In the 2000 election, Bush lost Pennsylvania while carrying West Virginia. Reelection had a greater probability if the president were able to win the electoral votes of Pennsylvania, the nation's leading producer of steel. Rove counseled the president to protect the industry's competitiveness on the world market and shore up support for the Bush campaign in Pennsylvania. According to Rove, the decision was also driven by a need to develop a bipartisan coalition to win fast-track trade promotion authority for the executive office.

"We're a group that wants to go as fast as possible," he said.

The president obliged, ignoring the hypocrisies of the decision. In spite of his support for a free market philosophy, embodied in the North American Free Trade Agreement (NAFTA), and later the Central American Free Trade Agreement (CAFTA) in his second term, Bush agreed to assess tariffs on imported steel. The duties keep the more expensively produced American steel on a price par with the less costly imports from nations like Japan. Steel import tariffs blatantly contradicted the president's campaign speeches about free markets, but they tactically improved his reelection chances in key industrial swing states and also moved votes in his direction for trade promotion powers. In the end, Bush may won a second term, and the purchasers of new automobiles wound up making larger car payments—all the result of strategy and influence exercised by Karl Rove on the world's most powerful office, the U.S. presidency.

Karl Rove, a solitary citizen, unelected, now has the kind of power in government and politics never before granted to a private citizen. In Texas, where Rove's work transformed the state's power structure, those defeated by the consultant are apprehensive over how he has gathered his authority and how it might be abused.

Soundly drubbed by Rove and his client, George W. Bush, in the 1998 gubernatorial race in Texas, Garry Mauro is convinced Karl Rove and his tactics have corrupted the democratic process.

"Yeah, I think he's an evil man. See, when we [Democrats] had the U.S. attorneys and the FBI, we didn't go sit down with the FBI and tell 'em to go get somebody. Karl Rove thought that was always okay. And that's why I think he's evil. He corrupts the system in a basic way."

Before he reached the White House, Rove left some unsettling signs on the landscape of Texas politics. He is connected to an apparently fraudulent bugging incident in his own office. Publicity surrounding the story, perfectly timed for maximum political effect, the day of the first gubernatorial debate and one month ahead of the 1986 vote, appears to have turned the election. Rove's client, former Governor Bill Clements, won—defeating Democrat Mark White, who was seeking reelection.

An ephemeral Rove also shows up in the periphery of a federal investigation of the Texas Department of Agriculture. His client, Rick Perry, who, ultimately, became the governor of Texas, was seeking to be elected agriculture commissioner, his first statewide office. Jim Hightower, the Democratic incumbent, was served with subpoenas the day he had planned for his reelection announcement. The subpoenas were based on files arguably delivered to an FBI agent by Larry Beauchamp, an investigator with the Travis County district attorney's office who had previously worked for Rick Perry's brother-in-law. Rove knew the FBI agent, Greg Rampton, from the earlier bugging investigation.

The day Rampton showed up at the Agriculture Department with the subpoenas, the Democrats of Texas turned their angry eyes to Rove.

Unfortunately, the political bullet meant for Democrat Hightower went wide of its mark, instead striking key administrators. Mike Moeller, deputy agriculture commissioner, and Pete McRae, another senior manager in the agency, were both indicted, along with three others, even though previous investigations by the state auditor and the U.S. Department of Agriculture found no violations of law. A compelling amount of narrative and files, some of it related to Karl Rove, built a significant case that the Texas Agriculture Department's executive staff were the objects of an orchestrated political assault. Exhibits not entered into evidence in the trial, along with other state and federal records that have never before been publicly revealed, are presented later in this book.

Rove has always worked best while hiding behind a curtain.

Episodes of dirty tricks, well-timed investigations, and electoral legerdemain, have turned Karl Rove into a political enigma and icon of campaign accomplishment. The idea that President George W. Bush simply does the bidding of his consultant is an obvious simplification. But it is just as foolish to ignore the manifest ways in which Rove has redefined the role of political advisor. The president may arrive at his own conclusions about politics and policy. But virtually all of the data, and its interpretation, are coming from Karl Rove. And the material, undoubtedly, points the president where his expert wants him to go on matters of both politics and policy.

In an evolutionary chart of the political consultant, Rove represents a new species of advisor. He is the product of the permanent campaign, the co-president, whose relationship with Bush, and his faithful guidance, have put him at the heart of power in a manner unknown to previous political consultants and U.S. electoral history.

Rove dismisses the notion that he is unique in American politics. He points to other precedents. But in virtually every case, past consultants have had a more circumscribed authority or, more typically, went away after their client took office. Not Rove. The consultant's role, based on his record, appears to be the business of getting the candidate elected, helping to steer policy while in office, assisting the officeholder's reelection, and using the second term to tee up the ball for the party's chosen successor. These are tasks that used to be the province of the candidate, who ultimately became the office-holder. The advent of the permanent campaign, however, a product of two decades of bitter presidential races, provided Rove the opportunity to alter the consultant's profile. He has created the permanent consultant. This new political creature brings with it implications Americans have yet to measure.

An amateur historian, Rove styled the Bush campaign after the work of Mark Hanna, an industrialist at the turn of the twentieth century. Hanna, who was more of an outside expert than a consultant, counseled William McKinley to ignore the post-Civil War influences on the electorate. His argument, which proved prescient, was that America was creating a new working class and economy as a result of industrialization and those people would vote on jobs and the future, not on associations lingering from the war. Similar visionary thinking by Rove, about the transformation of the Republican Party and twenty-first century demographics, lifted his premier client to the White House and reconfigured the role of political consultant.

Rove's choice of Hanna as an icon to represent his efforts with Bush is more revealing than has been considered. An industrialist, Hanna was best known for resisting government efforts to break up the giant trusts being developed by corporate and mining interests. These financial behemoths were able to control labor and wages with oppressive power. Hanna turned to the trusts to raise a record $4 million for the McKinley campaign, which made victory impossible for his Democratic opponent, William Jennings Bryan. For Bush, Rove used the same tactic, generating cash donations from corporate America for the Republican, in an amount that was unheard of in the history of American politics.

Hanna treated labor seriously, but not equally. While arguing he was willing to talk to laborers to improve their situations, Hanna's concerns, like Rove and Bush, were for business, assuming if big companies did well, everyone else would, too. According to the New York Times in 1896, that is not the way things turned out.

"The secretary of the Cleveland Central Labor Union wrote that Mr. Hanna had wrecked the Seaman's union of the lower lake regions (sic) that he had smashed the union of his street railway employees, and refuses to allow them to organize. Further, Mr. Hanna had assisted in destroying the mineworker's unions of Pennsylvania, and had tried to break up the carpenter's unions of Cleveland by employing nonunion men on his mansion at a critical time last spring, when the eight-hour law was being put into effect."

This then, was Rove's example of whom you needed to be to get things done. And for Bush and Rove, it has worked. Massive amounts of campaign money meant votes and then power. They won. But has democracy also lost something?

In the fullness of his accomplishments, Karl Rove has raised a new and disturbing question for American voters and their republic: Who really runs this country?

1

Off to the Show

The ring always believes that the finger lives for it.
—Malcom de Chazal

Wayne Slater, Austin bureau chief of the *Dallas Morning News*, stepped outside of a rope line to make sure Karl Rove had no trouble finding him in the crowd. Until that moment, Slater had been inconspicuous among the supporters and journalists gathered on the airport tarmac in Manchester, New Hampshire. The correspondent assumed Texas Governor George W. Bush's senior strategist was certainly going to be present when his boss arrived on a charter flight from Iowa for the debate at WMUR-TV. He knew Rove wanted to discuss the story he had written for that morning's edition of the Dallas paper.

Slater hardly saw Rove approach. Whether from the chill air or his anger, Rove's face was pink as it hovered inches away from the reporter. His index finger swung like a saber across Slater's chest.

"You're trying to ruin me," Rove charged. "My reputation. You son-of-a-bitch. It's my reputation."

"What are you talking about?"

Slater did not immediately connect Rove's anger with the story he had written for the paper that day. The intensity was out of proportion to what Slater perceived as a minor piece of reporting.

"That story, damn you. It's wrong. You're trying to ruin my reputation."

"Karl, everything I wrote is true."

"No, it isn't, you son of a bitch."

The two moved closer together, their coat lapels practically brushing, displaying the kind of overt anger that might abruptly turn physical. Slater reminded Rove they had previously discussed these matters, specifically, his dirty tricks as a young Republican.

"No, no, no! It's wrong."

Rove's finger was punching Slater firmly in the chest.

"Look, Karl, you forget it was me you kept calling about the FBI and the ag commissioner and what he was doing. You called me about the railroad commissioner's degree problem. You can say whatever you want to these other guys, but you can't deny this stuff to me. You were calling me. It was you and me, buddy."

Slater lightly touched Rove's chest with his index finger, as the consultant had done to him.

"Don't you touch me," Rove sputtered.

The extreme reaction did not make sense. Rove was fairly practiced at anger management and was more likely to slice up reporters with an intellectually condescending rebuke. Probably, the consultant was edgy because it was the day of the 2000 Republican Presidential Primary's initial debate. In Rove's mind, it must have seemed like the stars were lining up precisely as he had ordered. The Dallas story was a blemish on the face of Rove's beautifully executed campaign plan. There was no other explanation for his response. Two of Slater's colleagues watched in astonishment as Rove continued his rant, inches from the reporter's nose.

"You son-of-a-bitch. You said I taught dirty tricks."

"You did, Karl."

"No, no, no."

"The *Washington Post* reported it, Karl."

Slater reminded Rove that he had never protested a profile he had written months before, which referred to the *Post* story.

"They said it. A newspaper said it, okay. But you wrote that I flat-out did it."

"Well, that's because you did."

"A newspaper said I did."

Rove knew that the story was certain to be picked up by a growing group of national reporters who, from now on, would simply state that Rove was a master of dirty tricks. In his view, nobody had ever proved he was involved in campaign skullduggery. A newspaper had reported it, yes, but his opponents based their belief that Rove had used dirty tricks on unsubstantiated allegations in a political race years ago as a young Republican.

Slater pressed the issue. Rove did not deny the dirty tricks as a young Republican, but he continued to insist the Dallas story went too far.

"You son-of-a-bitch. You stay away from me," he hissed at Slater. "I'm not going to let you ruin my reputation."

Slater, left conspicuously alone between the rope lines as Rove abruptly stalked off, shrugged and moved toward the candidate coming from the plane. Less than a half hour later, inside the small general aviation terminal at the Manchester airport, he encountered Rove again.

"Hey, how's it goin'?" Slater asked.

"I'm fine," Rove answered.

Already, the strategist was moving on to more pressing matters. The confrontation with Slater was just another campaign event, part strategy, part emotion. Karl Rove has a fine eye for working journalists up to the edge, bullying and cajoling, and then pulling back. Rove had made his point. In the future, the reporter, and those in the campaign press corps watching from a few feet away, might exercise more caution when writing about him.

Rove was incapable of ignoring the *Dallas Morning News* piece or the journalist who had filed the copy. Jumping Slater was on his list of tasks for that day, along with getting his candidate in a final state of readiness for his first national debate.

Rove actually had sufficient reasons to be upbeat and pleased with the status of his candidate's campaign on that December day in 1999. Governor Bush was arriving in New Hampshire for the debate after an inspiring trip through Iowa. People, drawn by simple curiosity as well as political inclinations, had turned out in large, enthusiastic numbers to see the Texas governor. But not much of it was spontaneous. Rove was at the controls and nothing, therefore, happened without his advice and consent. No one had ever run a presidential campaign as meticulously as Karl Rove.

The energetic rallies with hay bales and music and the growing support for George W. Bush were not simply a democracy's response to the candidate's appeal. They were also the results of the plan being unfolded by Bush's senior political advisor. Rove was a strategist who was changing the process with his ideas. His gift, perhaps more than any political advisor in history, was the ability both to visualize the broad design of a successful presidential campaign and to manage its every detail.

"Karl just dominates this," said a Republican admirer from Texas. "Who's writing the scripts? Karl. Who's sitting there editing the film? Karl. Who's overseeing the media buy? Karl. Karl says do this and you do it. That's how he did it at Karl Rove and Company in Texas, and that's how he'll do it electing somebody president of the United States."

A man whose round face and thinning hair suggest more of a mailroom clerk than one of history's most intense political minds, Rove was in the midst of executing a 50-million-dollar maneuver to make sure his candidate won the Republican nomination for president. And voters were behaving according to plan.

The standard of performance for political advisors like Rove allows few chances at redemption. You either win your first time out, or you are gone from the profession. Winners turn into gurus, who then focus their attention on more stately challenges within the White House, or they leave their candidate to the affairs of state and move into private business and become highly paid experts. Losers are not first choices for candidates making an initial run.

Karl Rove was not a loser, at least not back in Texas. But he had never managed a presidential campaign either. And among Bush family loyalists, there were some lingering questions about whether his successes in state elections translated to a grander national scale. Rove took little or no notice of his skeptics. They did not have his gift for seeing the inevitable outcome. They did not understand his ability to control the variables.

Rove watched it all unfold in his head, long before it took place in the voting booths of Iowa. Each element of the Bush Iowa operation was poised and ready for competition on caucus day. Rove knew how to make farmers come in from the cold fields and drafty barns, get in their pickups and drive the snowy country roads into town to vote for George W. Bush. The intuition and detailed planning that had marked all of his previous political wins was guiding him through his first Republican presidential primary season as the top strategist of Bush.

Even the best make mistakes, though. Trouble was afoot in New Hampshire and Rove's finely tuned antennae were not picking up the signals. Iowa was a state where money and structure were a sound formula for predictable results. New Hampshire was more susceptible to a grass roots uprising. Candidates had almost enough time to shake the hand of each primary voter. The less complex dynamics were allowing Senator John McCain to surge in the state that hosted the first primary and Rove did not see the dark horizon. Mistakenly, the Bush campaign had misjudged McCain's frequent trips to New Hampshire during the previous August. In Iowa, Rove did not consider McCain to be a significant threat because of his opposition to federal subsidies for gasohol production from corn. McCain also lacked any type of field organization so critical in the caucuses.

Rove was overconfident. Two months from the New Hampshire vote, he was under the impression the situation was comfortably in hand. As his candidate campaigned across the state, Rove stepped up the media buy to a level that could not be matched by McCain. Tracking polls looked good and none of the intense background checks of Governor Bush by various media had led to damaging information. Rove felt he and his candidate had little left to do except execute the plan. The primary had become pro forma.

There were annoyances, like that day's story in the *Dallas Morning News*, but Rove dealt with such minor disturbances in an expeditious fashion. The Lee Atwater and Karl Rove approach for new political operatives, mentioned in Slater's story, was first reported in a 1973 *Washington Post* article. There was not much new in Slater's piece. The story, even in the estimation of the author, bordered on innocuous.

As Slater and other journalists traveling on the Bush Campaign knew, using operatives to attack opponents, leaking harmful information, or turning rumors into weapons, as was being done against McCain, was not a new tactic for Karl Rove. If traveling reporters did not know how Rove had used those tactics in the past, they did now. In campaigns at the state level, he had also used surrogates to blast opponents with leaks, whisper campaigns, and rumors while his clients remained above the fray. A Rove candidate was always able to honestly argue that he was running a clean, issues-oriented campaign because Rove stirred up the dirt without involving his client. He made phone calls to reporters, supplied documents, and produced third-party groups with damaging allegations. This approach, already a template for the modern electoral campaign, was refined by Rove with a deadly new precision.

After his confrontation with Slater, Rove left the Manchester airport in the governor's motorcade, a row of dark Suburbans chasing police cruisers with flashing lights through the snow and rock of New Hampshire. Anyone who knew him or had worked around him knew what Rove was thinking about. Certainly, he was looking ahead to that night's debate. But the heated exchange with the reporter must have still lingered in his mind. Rove knew the big picture was infinitely more important than a Texas journalist writing what he considered recycled copy. No one was allowed to damage the plan Karl Rove had been building for almost a quarter century, especially not a local reporter.

Rove understood that journalists were not so much opposition as referees. Dealing with them asked little of his great intellect. True political opponents, however, were a different kind of game, and Rove brought them down with the fervor of a natural predator.

"The playing field was always different for Karl," an adversary said. "There were no out-of-bounds markers for him. He'd do anything he had to, to win, even if that meant destroying your livelihood. A lot of times, it wasn't enough for Karl to just win. He had to crush you in the process."

The Texas political landscape was spotted with the blood of those who had been taken down by Karl Rove, and they, more than anyone in America, were confident George W. Bush was on his way to becoming president of the United States.

Karl Rove knew it, too. He knew something else, as well. This might not be only about George W. Bush. If he intended to play the role of high-profile political consultant, Rove needed to have answers for controversial matters in his own past. There were stories and allegations about things he had done. Eventually, reporters would hear about them. And then he would be the one answering questions. They were coming, no doubt about that. He just had to figure out what the answers were before he was asked. And hope his own past was of no risk to his candidate.

2

Consultant, Bug Thyself

All deception in the course of life is indeed nothing else but a lie reduced to practice, and falsehood passing from words into things.
—Robert Southey

With George W. Bush reelected to a second term, trust in the institutions of government, already beleaguered as a result of decades of high profile scandals, appeared to be low enough to threaten the future of important Democratic institutions. Evidence indicated various federal agencies were altering news releases and crunching data for political impact. Unemployment and manufacturing statistics were frequently revised without notice after they had made their monthly headlines. Facts about global warming were turned into topics for debate in spite of overwhelming scientific data. A governmental rule allowing clear cutting of trees instead of managed growth on public lands was cynically referred to as the "Healthy Forests Initiative" while a curtailment of EPA restrictions on factory emissions was named the "Clear Skies Initiative." The president kept connecting Iraq to 9/11 and in spite of bombings that killed dozens of people at a time in Baghdad, rising U.S. casualties, a flawed Iraqi constitution, and a dawning civil war, he insisted on telling Americans, "We're making progress in Iraq." And a government that said we were at risk because of weapons of mass destruction (WMD) was clearly implicated in exposing the name of an undercover CIA agent working in the area of WMD.

Anyone who trusted the government was mistrusted themselves. Some of this can be traced back to Vietnam and Watergate and the lies of Iran-Contra and President Clinton's parsing the language to obscure his sexual indiscretions. But all of those deceptions resulted in political repercussions. Justice has been slow to knock on the door of the Bush administration, however, and lying and misrepresentation have become conventional political tactics. The entire infrastructure of government has been reconfigured to serve political ends instead of taxpayers.

How did it get this way? Karl Rove is largely responsible for changing the rules and making untruths political assets. He has practiced deception from the beginning of his political career when he taught lessons in dirty tricks. And he has been wildly successful at escaping recrimination. Before he took off for the White House to alter the way elections were conducted in America, Rove was plying his dark craft in Texas.

And he was good at it from the first day.

For almost seven hours on a Sunday afternoon in 1986, security experts swept two offices of the Bill Clements for Governor Campaign. They were looking for bugging devices but had, thus far, found nothing. Convinced there were no illegal transmitters in the main office, the two-man team moved to the suites owned by Karl Rove, the governor's campaign strategist.

Gary L. Morphew, owner of Knight Diversified Services, and Bruce Wayne Scott, one of his 60 employees, were conducting the search. As evening approached, Scott said he stepped out of the offices to take a break, leaving Morphew alone with the job. Scott claimed that when he walked back in, Morphew was unscrewing switch plates from the wall and taking the phone apart.

"It wouldn't surprise me if we found a bug in this place," Scott remembered Morphew telling him.

Karl Rove and Company, a political consulting firm, was heavily involved in the second gubernatorial campaign of Republican Bill Clements. The private security company was called in to conduct the sweep because Rove and Clements' campaign manager, George Bayoud, had become convinced that proprietary information about their strategy had leaked to reporters, and the campaign staff of Democratic opponent, incumbent Governor Mark White.

"There have been a number of instances over the summer when sensitive issues about campaign strategy have become known," Rove said. "It's been eerie, too much on target, items that have been very closely held."

Scott said that after returning from his break, he continued his check of the space using a device called a Hound Dog, which is a field-strength gauge for measuring radio frequency transmissions. Scott reported nothing was registering on the meter.

"I'm not picking up anything on this, Gary," he said.

"I don't think you're doing it right," Morphew responded, according to Scott. "Let me show you how to reset, and then you can redo your sweep."

Scott said that after recalibrating the Hound Dog, Morphew left him alone in the room to finish the frequency scan.

This time, Scott located an electronic bug behind a picture frame above Karl Rove's desk, close enough to have picked up and transmitted all of Rove's phone conversations. Hidden on the frame of a red, white, and blue needlepoint of the GOP elephant, the transmitter had a short wire antenna and, according to later tests, was able to send radio signals up to a half mile in open air.

The bug was found at 7:40 P.M. on Sunday, October 5, 1986, and Jaime Clements, who is not related to the candidate, was the only Rove and Company employee in the building. Morphew and Scott informed Clements of the discovery.

"Turn it off and get it the hell out of here," Clements told the men, according to Morphew.

Morphew said he told Clements that authorities are not normally contacted when a transmitter is discovered. He said either he, or Rove and Company, could dispose of the bug. Scott later told investigators he was convinced Morphew did not believe the results of the sweep would be reported to law enforcement. The two men returned to their hotel rooms with the device.

Karl Rove, though, called the police. According to Texas Department of Public Safety (DPS) records, Rove contacted that agency a few minutes after 11:00 P.M. Sunday. He also phoned the U.S. attorney's office and the Travis County district attorney. The DPS's initial incident report said Rove claimed he was called by the FBI, and was told to secure the area. He said that bureau investigators told him they would be on the premises in the morning.

In the interim, Rove had Morphew and Scott come back to his office from their hotel and bring the device. Around midnight, two representatives of the Travis County district attorney's office arrived at Karl Rove and Company headquarters. They took possession of the bug and stored it in a safe at the DA's office in the Travis County Courthouse. Rove ordered the two private investigators, Morphew and Scott, to spend the night at his office. Morphew spent much of that time writing a statement about the discovery and disposition of the device, which he presented to the DPS the next morning. There were contradictions between Morphew's and Scott's description of events, including Morphew's denial he was ever alone in Rove's office.

As a state forensics team carried out its investigation, FBI agent Greg Rampton arrived at Rove's offices. DPS commanders on the scene decided to turn the bug over to Rampton to have the federal labs in Washington, DC, do an extensive analysis of the device's operation and technology. A slender man with graying blonde hair,

Rampton's name was to appear in Austin newspapers many times in coming years. Rampton eventually led investigations into nearly every statewide Democratic officeholder in Texas during his tenure in the Austin office of the FBI.

Rove had a quick and ready answer when asked about potential suspects, and it was, predictably, political. His perceptions were detailed in the FBI's incident report, apparently written by Special Agent Byron Sage a few days later, and relayed to the FBI director's office in Washington, DC:

ROVE AND CLEMENTS' CAMPAIGN DIRECTOR GEORGE BAYOUD DECIDED TO SEARCH FOR A "BUG" FOLLOWING A TELEPHONE CONVERSATION BETWEEN THE TWO ON MONDAY, 9/29/86, WHEN THEY DISCUSSED THE POSSIBILITY OF LEE ATWATER, AIDE TO VICE PRESIDENT BUSH, BEING BROUGHT IN TO HELP THE CLEMENTS CAMPAIGN DURING ITS LAST 30 DAYS AND A DECISION TO INCREASE CLEMENTS' TV ADVERTISING BUY TO 650 GROSS RATINGS POINTS. ACCORDING TO ROVE, THIS INFORMATION WAS MENTIONED BY DALLAS MORNING NEWS REPORTER SAM ATTLESEY IN A CONVERSATION WITH CLEMENTS' PRESS SECRETARY REGGIE BASHUR ON 9/30/86 AND ATTLESEY SAID HIS SOURCE WAS HARRIS DIAMOND, A POLITICAL CONSULTANT TO CLEMENTS' OPPONENT, TEXAS GOVERNOR MARK WHITE. AS A RESULT, THE SEARCH WAS AUTHORIZED.

"Checking my office was an afterthought," Rove said in an interview more than a decade and a half later. "Bayoud hired him to sweep the headquarters because the thought was it was in the headquarters. So, he was literally sent over to our office as an afterthought."

The notion that checking his office was an "afterthought" contradicted Rove's own recollections of the incident, at the time. Why would it have been an afterthought to sweep his office when Rove claimed that was the specific location where the private conversation took place?

"Are you sure it [the conversation] wasn't on the phone?" he was asked, when questioned in 2002.

"Maybe it's on the phone. I can't remember. But it's something in my office. I can't remember what it was. But there's only one conversation where that number [gross ratings points] is discussed and it's in my office."

There does not appear to be any reasonable explanation as to why the security team was sent first to campaign headquarters and then to Rove's office when, by Rove's own recounting, the Clements' team was convinced the leak came from Rove's place.

The "afterthought," though, led to some forward thinking.

Rove's instinct was to turn every circumstance into a political advantage. The only debate of the 1986 Texas gubernatorial race was to be held that night in Houston. If news about the bug spread widely enough, it might disrupt Democrat Mark White's debate preparations and overshadow any story lines critical of Rove's Republican candidate. Potential gaffes by Rove's client, Bill Clements—always a worry on debate night—might get secondary play in the next day's papers. The big story would be the bugging.

As October began, the Clements campaign was struggling. None of its issues had sufficient traction with voters and the incumbent governor, Mark White, was closing the gap between himself and his Republican opponent. Independent polls at midsummer had shown White trailing Clements by 20 points. By October, White had cut this lead in half.

A member of the Republican campaign's group of advisors admitted their candidate was in need of an issue or a weapon. "Tactically, they ran a better campaign; they had better TV. I remember White attacked us all summer. And Clements didn't want to spend the money. And White basically caught up. So it was a close race."

Even to the uninitiated, it was clear the controversy over finding a secret listening device would help Clements. Hastily, Rove began to make plans for a news conference in his office. A reasonable number of TV crews showing up also meant that the early newscasts would be talking about the bugging, instead of the debate. Correspondents would not be previewing the debate, creating unrealistic expectations, talking about issues that might prove troubling for the Republican.

After reporters arrived, Rove laid out a tale of political espionage involving a hidden wireless microphone, secretly transmitting from his office. He got up and pointed at a framed needlepoint of a red, white, and blue elephant, the GOP mascot, on the wall. Rove explained that a transmitter, about the size of a matchbox, had been discovered attached to the frame of the needlepoint, only four feet from where he spoke regularly on the telephone.

"So, who do you think is responsible for this, Karl?" a reporter asked.

"Obviously, I do not know who did this, but there is no doubt in my mind that the only ones who could have benefited from this detailed, sensitive information, would have been the political opposition."

The air was acidic with skepticism as Rove told his story. Afterwards, reporters speculated whether the bugging was a political stunt pulled off by Rove or Republican operatives. The most dubious of the crowd was veteran political writer Sam Attlesey of the Dallas Morning News. Attlesey's detailed questions of Rove and the Clements' campaign managers had supposedly prompted Rove and Bayoud to hire the security firm. They claimed he had information from the Democrat camp that could have only come from the Clements campaign. Attlesey was blunt at the news conference.

"How do we know you didn't just put it there yourself, Karl?" Attlesey asked. "You know, just so you could call a news conference and talk about it."

"Well, Sam, I guess you don't," Rove answered. "But it doesn't really make any sense for me to bug myself, does it?"

"How long do you suppose it had been there on the picture frame?" a television reporter asked.

"It could have been there at least for the past four days. But it could have been there, and likely was there, for a lot longer. I just don't know."

Rove apparently had been away from his office for the past four days. But one date he remembered exactly—the date he had last looked behind the needlepoint frame. August 6, he recalled. Rove said during the news conference that he had removed the piece of artwork from the wall on that date because he had considered replacing it with another picture but decided against the change. Even with a mind fueled by minutiae, the ability to recall a specific date from two months earlier about such an inconsequential act seemed, if not suspicious, at the very least, oddly precise. Rove has always practiced selective recall for political effect. When an investigation about the leak of a CIA agent's name began during the second Bush administration, Rove had trouble recalling what reporters he had spoken with about the agent, if any, and specifically what he had said to them.

As always, Rove's words during the session with reporters were very carefully measured for maximum impact. Despite a sharp flurry of questioning, he never overtly accused the Democratic governor of doing anything illegal. His responses left open the possibility that someone in Mark White's campaign might have done this without the governor's knowledge—a rogue operative, maybe. At the same time, Rove did not discount the possibility that White might have been aware of the bugging.

The media response was precisely what Rove might have anticipated. Representatives were present from each of the major newspapers in the state's four largest cities: the *Dallas Morning News*, *Dallas Times Herald*, *Houston Chronicle*, *Houston Post*, *Austin American-Statesman*, *Fort Worth Star-Telegram*, and the *San Antonio Express-News*. A full complement of television crews was also in attendance. The five and six o'clock newscasts on KPRC-TV, Houston, and WFAA-TV, Dallas, the two pre-eminent newscasts in Texas, led with live reports from their Austin correspondents. Also, KDFW-TV, Dallas-Fort Worth; KXAS-TV, Fort Worth; KTRK-TV, Houston; and

KTVV-TV, Austin, sent reporter and photographer teams to Rove's news conference.

Inevitably, the story distracted from advance coverage of the debate and any reporting on issues confronting the state. Editors will pick a mystery over a policy discussion every time.

The debate between Mark White and Bill Clements went on as scheduled, broadcast statewide, and no questions were asked about the bugging. But after the camera lights went off, reporters in the studio flocked to the two candidates to ask questions about the debate and the listening device.

"Well, I was surprised," Clements told reporters. "I was disappointed. I was shocked."

Clearly, Rove and the ex-governor had talked about the episode.

Suddenly faced with implications that he might be connected to the bugging episode, the incumbent governor, normally a subdued campaigner, stood before a battery of cameras, his face flushed with anger.

"I don't know anything about it, and I would hope they wouldn't suggest we had anything to do with it," White said. "Obviously, we didn't."

The bugging did do political harm. The late Matt Lyon, who was Governor White's speechwriter, later told his friend, Patricia Tierney Alofsin, that White got news of the bugging at precisely the wrong time.

"Mark White got word right before they went on for the debate. I know all this through Matt. Matt told me that Mark White was told all about this minutes before going on, and it just really rattled him. And he didn't give a very good performance. If you go back and look at that debate, it was terrible. It was really from that moment on that things started going not so well for Mark White."

Tuesday morning's papers, not surprisingly, gave the bugging story prominent play, overwhelming the coverage of the debate. The Republican and Democratic campaigns released operatives to put their spin on the story. The main media liaison for the White camp was Mark McKinnon, who some years later switched to the Republican Party and joined the legions of Karl Rove admirers. More than a decade later, McKinnon became part of the Texas team that put Bush in the White House and became a senior adviser to the President during both Bush terms. On the day of the bug's discovery, however, his Democratic taproot was still deep in its political soil.

"If they found a bug, that's a serious matter. But if they are blaming us, it's a bunch of bull. It is outrageous and sad that Rove would suggest the White campaign would be involved in a matter like this. The entire matter is both bizarre and incredible."

Early indications, in follow-up stories, were that the Republicans intended to press hard and use the bugging as an issue to question the credibility and trustworthiness of the Democrats. Reggie Bashur, Clements' media spokesperson, told Anne Marie Kilday of the *Houston Chronicle* that the bugging of Rove's office was a sad milestone for Texas politics.

"Whoever thought Watergate-style politics would come to the Lone Star state? It's happened. It's Texasgate."

Bashur's comments were an indication the Republicans planned to use the Rove bugging incident to grind down the White campaign. They had a controversial issue they could use to batter the Democrat. Why wouldn't they use it? And use it every day. But something happened to cause Rove and his team to go quiet on the bugging.

The investigation ended up making suspects out of Rove and the Republicans instead of the Democrats.

3

Politically Paranormal

There he goes. One of God's own prototypes. Some kind of high-powered mutant never even considered for mass production. Too weird to live and too weird to die.

—Hunter S. Thompson

Things were not happening the way they were supposed to for Karl Rove. The security company hired by the Clements campaign had damaged his reputation. The way the firm handled the discovery of a bug in Rove's office had led to an endless assault of questions from lawmen, reporters, and Democrats. The way Knight Diversified Services and the Clements campaign handled the situation prompted the nickname, "Goobergate."

Suddenly, and without explanation, Republicans dropped the controversy as a campaign issue. Whatever the early political advantage, a series of bungled decisions began to make people doubt the Republicans more than the Democrats.

A Republican campaign operative, who assisted the Clements team, still has questions about the affair.

"And we got this firm out of Fort Worth. And I asked why did you go to Fort Worth? And, it's, well, they discovered it. So, I'm buying this, hook, line, and sinker. And we're pushing this four, five days. And the next day, I wake up, all right, listen. And . . . says, well listen, we may want to tone this down. And I say what? And Karl says that's enough, that's enough. And the tracking shows the Mark White advance stalls, and actually reverses. We did a great job."

The most troubling aspect of the case, however, for both law enforcement and the Clements campaign, was the disposition of the electronic device after the Hound Dog meter had found it. Even an amateur sleuth would have thought to leave the bug in place, feed it phony information and then wait for a source to use that false material.

When security firm hired by Rove removed the bug from the wall frame, it eliminated the best chance of finding the interloper. The action became the subject of dispute by political interests and law enforcement agencies. Gary Morphew's decision on how to handle the bug had the effect of turning him into a suspect. In his statement to investigators, Morphew, who owned the security company, said he was ordered to get the device out of the office by Rove employee Jaime Clements.

Clements denied that.

"I told them to do what it is they do," Clements told reporters, who began calling him repeatedly. "I certainly do not recall telling them to turn it off and get it out of the office."

Morphew disagreed with Jaime Clements' characterization of why the bug was taken back to Morphew and Scott's hotel room.

"I removed that device at the direction of their people," he told the DPS and FBI. "I did nothing illegal or wrong."

Under pressure from the Clements campaign, Morphew also said he was willing to sit for the lie detector. However, when arrangements were made for the test, he changed his mind and refused for what he called, "personal reasons." "I have no legal or moral requirements to take it. I don't have to, and I am not going to," declared Morphew to the Austin American-Statesman.

Two weeks later, Texas newspapers were still writing about Morphew's decisions and the episode in Rove's office. In an interview with Guillermo X. Garcia of the *Austin American-Statesman*, Dave Logan, a former federal investigator from Dallas, was among the most critical of Morphew's Knight Diversified Services.

"I can tell you that just about any professional would have handled the situation different. An investigator who is paid good money should be able to advise the client about options, the legalities involved, who enforces the appropriate criminal statutes, how to preserve the scene as evidence, things like that. I damn sure would not have removed it to a motel room without even contacting authorities, the FBI, which has the jurisdiction."

Results of the FBI lab work in Washington only added confusion. According to tests, the battery was a six-volt with 5.8 volts of remaining power. The life of the battery, however, caused the greatest problem for investigators. Maximum battery life was 10 hours. Obviously, this was evidence that whoever had placed the bug was someone with recurring access to change the battery, or someone who did not care if the device transmitted, only that it be found. Equally troubling, the residual life of the battery, at 5.8 volts, was irrefutable proof that the bug had been put in place and turned on the same day it had been discovered.

McKinnon, the Republican convert and compatriot of Rove's in both Bush presidential campaigns, implied during the 1986 campaign that Rove had planted the bug himself by referring to the Watergate break-in of 1972. "It seems to me the Republicans are the ones who have experience at this kind of stuff. I think this whole thing stinks, and I think that the wind is blowing from the Clements campaign."

Publicly, at least, there was one issue on which both the White and Clements campaigns concurred. Both sides felt removing the bug had been a mistake.

"I don't know why they took the bug with them to the hotel," Rove said. "But I am not going to second guess them. I believed it would have been useful to feed the bug information to see where that information surfaced."

McKinnon agreed.

"Why didn't they just leave the damn thing on and really put out some disinformation, and catch whoever it was red-handed?"

Officially, law enforcement looked at both campaigns and came to no conclusion. The FBI report, however, casts some doubt over Rove's and Bayoud's motivation for having a security company conduct a sweep.

The oft-repeated story from Karl Rove and campaign manager George Bayoud went like this: Information from a privileged, confidential telephone conversation they had on September 30, 1986, had gotten into the hands of *Dallas Morning News* reporter Sam Attlesey. During that call, the two said they discussed raising the Clements' media buy to 650 gross ratings points—a measure of how many people would see the commercial—as well as hiring consultant Lee Atwater for the final 30 days of the gubernatorial race. Attlesey first heard the information from Harris Diamond, a political consultant in Virginia, retained by the White campaign. Clements' staffers then told several Texas reporters that the only way Diamond could have acquired such information was through the bug in Rove's office.

According to Rove, during an interview years later, his suspicions of a leak were prompted by the confidential discussion with Bayoud of ratings points for the media buy. During that private conversation, Rove said, he gave the wrong number to Bayoud.

"Later that day I see Bayoud, I'm on my way to the Austin Club, and I say, 'George, I got the number wrong, the real number is X,' and then later that afternoon Bayoud calls me and says, 'I got a call from Sam or somebody about the number.' Well, I had misspoken the number. It's not like that was on a piece of paper anywhere that could have been circulated by anyone else. I literally say the number wrong. I say it right on the street. I correct it on the street. I say it's not what the number X was. Here's the real number. And so Bayoud then calls me that afternoon and says this is sort of weird that number you gave me this morning and says, in essence, 'Did you call anybody?'"

When he was interviewed by the FBI, Attlesey said that Harris Diamond never made any mention of "gross ratings points" or Lee Atwater. He spoke only in general terms of the firm in which Atwater was a partner, Stone, Black, Manafort and Atwater. Diamond also used the dollar figure of $650,000.00, not "gross ratings points." Diamond told investigators he got weekly canvassing reports from the Sawyer-Miller Group in New York City, which was producing television ads for the Mark White campaign. As it turned out, the secret information from the Clements camp might not have been so secret after all.

Rove, though, disputed that.

"We haven't placed a buy at that point. We're placing the buy. It's not fully placed. Whatever it was. There's no way anyone could have fully deduced that number."

The FBI's incident report on the Rove bugging had never before been published. The document dramatically contradicted Rove's rationale for having an electronic sweep performed in his office:

DIAMOND ADVISED THAT SOMETIME BETWEEN 9/26/86 AND 10/3/86 HE WAS TOLD BY THE SAWYER/MILLER GROUP THAT CLEMENTS HAD INCREASED HIS BUY FROM 450 TO 700 GROSS RATINGS POINTS FOR THE FIRST TIME. DIAMOND LATER RAN INTO ATTLESEY AT A LOCAL RESTAURANT AND MENTIONED IT TO HIM. ACCORDING TO DIAMOND, ATTLESEY ASKED HIM TO TRANSLATE 700 POINTS TO DOLLARS AND DIAMOND FIGURED THAT AT A RATE OF $70,000 TO $80,000 PER 100 POINTS THAT THE WHITE CAMPAIGN WAS PAYING 700 POINTS WOULD TOTAL $500,000 AND THE ADDITIONAL RADIO ADVERTISING TIME CLEMENTS WAS BUYING WOULD AMOUNT TO $150,000, GIVING A TOTAL OF $650,000. THIS IS THE FIGURE HE GAVE ATTLESEY.

Transmitted to the FBI director in Washington, investigators reported to the agency that it was easy to acquire the information through public sources. The FBI quickly concluded that neither Harris Diamond, nor anyone else, needed a hidden microphone to pick up details on Rove's media buy for the Clements campaign. All anyone needed was a telephone.

. . . IT APPEARS THAT THE INFORMATION THAT THE CLEMENTS CAMPAIGN STAFFERS FELT WAS CLOSELY HELD WAS, IN ACTUALITY, KNOWN BY THE WHITE CAMPAIGN THROUGH LEGITIMATE SOURCES AT ABOUT THE SAME PERIOD OF TIME. THE SIGNIFICANT FIGURE OF 650 GROSS RATINGS POINTS WHICH VICTIM ROVE GAVE GEORGE BAYOUD ON 9/29/86, WAS COINCIDENTALLY SIMILAR TO THE $650,000 FIGURE DERIVED FROM 700 GROSS RATING POINTS BY DIAMOND AND GIVEN TO NEWS REPORTER ATTLESEY.

So how did the bug end up in Karl Rove's office? Democrat Mark White's staffers believe Rove was the culprit. But because of the transmitter's short battery life, that means Rove had to have slipped clandestinely back into Austin, early Sunday morning, from his campaign trip, plant the bug, and then race back to Dallas. Unlikely, unless he had put it in place before leaving and an accomplice turned it on Sunday at Rove's direction. Maybe one of Rove's business or political opponents did it. The short battery life, though, suggested they would have had to breach security on a daily basis to keep the bug transmitting. And there's no evidence anyone had broken into Rove and Company headquarters. The battery's six hours of usefulness and the lack of any evidence indicating a break-in is a strong clue that, whoever planted the bug had easy, recurring access to Rove's office.

Suspicion, publicly, though, kept getting aimed at the surveillance company. The reluctance and, ultimately, the refusal of Gary Morphew, owner of the security firm, to take a polygraph exam also made him a key suspect. Even though he has consistently denied involvement in the bugging through the years, one of the Texas DPS investigators still thinks the evidence points to Morphew.

"I wouldn't quite call it an old policeman's intuition. But we had everything but a confession from the guy," said Tommy Davis, lead DPS investigator on the bugging.

A Texas Republican party insider who was closely involved in the 1986 campaign is still wondering what might be the truth. "Did Karl know about all this stuff, or didn't he know about it? The bug was in his office. I don't know if they discovered it or Karl discovered it. It's a good anecdote in the play-for-keeps department. Either [the Clements campaign] knew when they hired them that they would find it, or it was possible they [Knight Diversified Services] were promoting their own deal. We were very eager. Because we were in trouble. Mark White was winning that election, and we had to do something, and we jumped at what we thought was something."

Rove has insisted all along that he was never a suspect in the case. But an FBI source in Washington, speaking on condition of anonymity, said, from the beginning, the suspects were obvious and Rove was, indeed, at the top of the list. According to this person, who was close to the investigation, agents were immediately suspicious of Rove and the Clements campaign because of the timing and the technical specifications of the device and lack of evidence of a break-in. This investigator said all of those details made the bugging look like an inside job, which meant, in his assessment, that someone in the campaign planted the bug or they were working with the security firm to make sure a bug was discovered.

"We were completely aware of the dynamics of all of this. It was the day before the debate. It was toward the end of the election and it could affect a lot of things. It all pointed in an obvious direction. We just did not have time to prove it. There were more important things going on in Texas at that time."

Sixteen years after it happened, Rove was asked who he thought was responsible for planting the transmitter in his building.

"I have no idea. Look, there are a lot of weird people running around in politics, particularly in Austin, Texas, in the seventies and eighties. There are just a lot of crazy people."

Polls from the 1986 Texas gubernatorial election show that ubiquitous news coverage of the bugging altered Mark White's political fortunes. The steady increase in his support came to a quick stop, and then began to decline. Mark McKinnon, the Rove adversary turned associate, was told of the impact.

"The numbers show that when the bugging came out, he just stopped."

"He?" McKinnon asked.

"White."

"So, it worked."

Whatever the residual skepticism over the bugging incident, the affair had faded into the haze of Texas political lore until the 2000 presidential race. George W. Bush and, to a lesser extent, his chief strategist were suddenly the objects of great scrutiny. With a few exceptions, feature stories on Rove gave little or no attention to the bugging. Instead, they concentrated on making a case for the political wunderkind, his brilliance and vision, his command of the field of battle, and the Rove willingness to do whatever was necessary to win.

Rarely chatty with journalists, Rove succumbed, one evening while campaigning, to convivial talk about his chosen profession. Conversation centered on a movie involving political consulting that had captured Rove's imagination. Directed by Sidney Lumet, the film *Power* is about a high-profile, very successful political strategist, who travels around the country on private jets, winning campaigns.

The lead character, played by Richard Gere, lives in a pricey Manhattan high-rise, deftly manipulates the media, and determines the fate of candidates across the nation.

Rove loved the film for its absurdities.

"I mean what was important to me was, what was unbelievable, the guy flies around in his own private jet. Everybody pays him 25 grand a month, his offices are sleekly paneled in a New York high-rise, he has an unbelievably attractive secretary, who he has sex with in the shower, I mean, you know, that's what I remember, I don't remember the other stuff."

In his enthusiasm for the movie, Rove either overlooked or forgot the pivotal moment in the story's plot. Richard Gere's character, who is managing several campaigns, is talking on the phone in his production studio. As he approaches the video monitor to view a tape, while still conducting his phone conversation, he notices the picture flutters. He backs away and the screen stabilizes. Stepping close to the monitor again, he holds up the phone, and the picture, once more, flutters. The character immediately realizes that radio signals coming from his phone are causing distortion on his television screen. Unscrewing the cover on the mouthpiece, he finds a wireless transmitter, a bug.

The movie showed up in theatres early in 1986, months before the illegal electronic device was uncovered in the offices of Karl Rove and Company.

Asked about that coincidence, Rove said he had watched the movie on a VCR, many years after its release, and was probably not paying attention when the bugging scene was on.

"That's why it was probably on a VCR because, you know, I don't know about you, but I put the VCR in there, and I get phone calls or go get a . . . but I literally do not remember that part."

If Rove's campaigns are characterized by anything, it is his attention to detail and an exquisite sense of timing. There is an exact moment to attack and a right time to talk issues. He lays out a schedule and plotline with the same eye for detail as a movie producer. So the release of the film *Power* with its pivotal scene about campaign espionage just months before a similar episode played itself out for real in Rove's office—leveling the campaign of Democrat Mark White—had the look of extraordinary coincidence, at the very least.

A federal grand jury in Austin was presented all available evidence in the real-life bugging involving Karl Rove. Three months later, at approximately the time Rove's client, William P. Clements was being inaugurated; federal investigators conceded they did not have enough material evidence to indict anyone.

One summer night about a year after the bugging, Rove may have offered a glimpse of the facts. Political consultant John Weaver had invited Rove and his wife, Darby, to dinner. The Weavers had been friends of the Rove's for a long time. Weaver had worked on Clements' campaign, and now that Clements was governor, he and Rove had moved on to other projects.

Democrats and Republicans were working together to bring the Superconducting Supercollider to Texas. The giant atom smasher was the most important scientific project in the country and the campaign to bring it to Texas transcended political party.

Matt Lyon, the defeated governor's speechwriter, and his friend, Patricia Tierney Alofsin, were also invited to the small dinner party. At one point in the evening, Tierney Alofsin recalled, the subject of conversation turned to the bugging.

"Of course, Rove knew Matt had worked with Mark White. And there was some discussion about it. And Karl all but came out and said, 'I did it.' He was proud of it. It was sort of like, 'We really messed you over, didn't we?'"

Tierney Alofsin thought how odd it was to be sitting there so long after the fact, after all the fulsome denials and the wreckage it had made of White's campaign—and now Rove, grinning and ebullient, was acting as if he wanted to take credit for it. She considered getting up and leaving, but did not.

"I don't remember the exact words, but I remember being shocked," she said. "It was like those cases where people murder people, and then they leave clues because they do this fabulous murder, and they want the police to know they did it. It was that sort of thing. He was so proud of it."

Whenever he deconstructs campaigns of his past, Rove always talks about luck. He is consistently lucky. But how much luck can a political operative have? His office ends up being bugged and it gets discovered the day before the only debate of the campaign? Not even lucky Karl Rove is that lucky. And the bug is discovered in the same year that a movie about a political bugging is released and Rove wants people to believe that, too, is just coincidence.

Lucky Karl.

Whatever happened, it did not stick to him, even though, over the years, fingers have slowly pointed back in his direction. Rove has claimed that situations arise and he uses them to create better campaigns. But there is greater plausibility that Rove is responsible for generating the environments that provide advantage to his candidates. He never got publicly accused in the bugging of his own office. But it's hard to look elsewhere for the perpetrator, especially using Rove's own standard of, "Who had the most to gain?"

Karl Rove did.

4

Livin' with the Long Knives

There is no act of treachery or meanness of which a political
party is not capable; for in politics there is no honour.

—Benjamin Disraeli

In the Travis County district attorney's office, Larry Beauchamp
was launching an investigation of the Texas Department of Agriculture. He had called the office of the inspector general at the
regional headquarters of the U.S. Department of Agriculture
(USDA). As an investigator with the Public Integrity Unit of the
Travis County district attorney's office, Beauchamp was a member of
a marginally funded and understaffed operation tasked with watching over government agencies and elected officials. He asked for
records related to a USDA probe of Texas Agriculture Commissioner Jim Hightower.

A year earlier, questions had been asked about credit card expenditures of Hightower and members of his staff. As part of a
decades' old cooperative agreement with USDA, Texas ran a crop
inspection service operation and money generated covered the ex-
penses of managers. Credit cards used by employees were paid out
of an account that was not subject to standard state audits. Problems

39

for the operation began when an employee had suggested to Washington that there might have been indiscretions in how those credit cards were used.

Those problems became political when Karl Rove's client decided to run for agriculture commissioner.

Although USDA's internal audit found that "there are no apparent violations of federal laws or misuse of federal funds," Larry Beauchamp was seeking files from the final report. The records were likely to disappoint him or any other investigator. A summary, written by the regional inspector general, said, "The agency is very pleased with the program being carried out by Texas-Federal, in terms of quality and accuracy of the fruit and vegetable inspection work."

Beauchamp's curiosity, though, was probably not driven by the findings of the audit summary but what details might have been turned up in the process. Neither was Beauchamp without a possible political motive for his call. Before joining the Travis County district attorney's staff, Beauchamp had worked as an investigator for the district attorney in Haskell County, Texas, a man named Joseph Thigpen. Thigpen's sister Anita was married to Rick Perry, who, one month prior to Beauchamp's call to USDA, had announced he was switching to the Republican Party and contemplating a run for agriculture commissioner against Jim Hightower. His campaign manager was to be Karl Rove.

Beauchamp had become friends with the Perrys, who also came from Haskell County, and he was, quite possibly, looking for information in the USDA audit that might help Perry in a potential campaign against Hightower. Rove would know what to do with it. Campaigns did not need to prove allegations like auditors and lawyers.

Almost a year later, when he was confronted about his political affiliations and possible reasons for contacting USDA, Beauchamp did not shade his anger.

"To question my intentions and integrity on that is really offensive to me," he told *Austin American-Statesman* reporter David Elliot.

Beauchamp may have been acting on his own initiative but he did have political connections to the Republicans. Karl Rove, who had stepped in to guide Rick Perry's political future after the rancher left the Democratic Party, was also the head strategist for Republican Governor Bill Clements. Both Clements and Perry would be pleased by the demise of Agriculture Commissioner Jim Hightower. He was Perry's Democratic opponent in the coming election, if Perry chose to run for agriculture commissioner, and Clements had long despised Hightower for his nontraditional approach to agriculture.

Larry Beauchamp, while not officially a part of the Perry campaign, could have been acting as a Karl Rove surrogate. Beauchamp did not need authorization to launch his own investigation of the Texas agriculture department. It was common practice for investigators of the Travis County Public Integrity Unit to gather information when they heard allegations.

The requested files were forwarded to Beauchamp with a note that said, "We did not investigate this matter due to the absence of a provable federal violation." But Beauchamp may have had his own plans for the material. When asked by a reporter if he had turned them over to the FBI, he said, "It's possible."

A federal investigation of the Texas Department of Agriculture, Commissioner Jim Hightower had the potential to change the political landscape of Texas and feed Karl Rove's dreams. Nationally, leaders of the Republican Party despised Hightower. During a keynote speech at the Democratic National Convention in 1988, Hightower kept referring to George Herbert Walker Bush as "Georgie." In his most quoted line from the Atlanta meeting, Hightower said, "George Bush is the kind of guy who wakes up on third base and thinks he hit a triple."

Hightower's rhetorical skills were not the only annoyance. The attention he had begun to receive as a populist orator, particularly as a result of his Democratic National Convention speech, had him thinking he had a shot at knocking off Republican U.S. Senator

Phil Gramm of Texas. If, however, Hightower chose to run for re-election to agriculture commissioner instead of taking on Gramm, and Rove then was able to bring Hightower down with a Perry candidacy, Rove would be doing a favor for his party and the Bush family who he had been involved with since the early 1970s.

It would also serve a greater plan Rove was already formulating.

The task was hardly a simple one. In spite of Bill Clements' re-election, Texas was still a state where Democrats were in charge. They were proficient fund-raisers with sound organization and conservative policies. As 1990 approached, Democrats did not expect Rove and his party to gain more than a precarious foothold.

Pete McRae, who worked for Hightower said Democrats were confident and Rove's machinations did not cause them great concern.

"At that time, there were no reasonable hopes for them. All of our incumbents were well financed, much better than the opposition. The likelihood of a state rep like Rick Perry beating an incumbent like Hightower was considered highly remote. And not just by us but by the Republicans, too."

And then things started happening.

In the span of three days, political infrastructure began to deteriorate for Texas Democrats. On Halloween morning of 1989, Bruce Tomaso of the *Dallas Morning News* started a series of stories about credit card usage by agriculture department staffers.

The next morning Larry Beauchamp made his call to the USDA, seeking records of the agency's audit of Texas-Federal.

Forty-eight hours later, Kenneth Boatwright, a former agriculture department division director, who worked for Hightower, announced his candidacy, implying corruption was afoot within the agency. Boatwright had consulted with Karl Rove before making his decision.

And Thomas Wall, the USDA official contacted by Beauchamp, also took a call from an Austin FBI agent.

"And I furnished him the exact same type of information that I furnished Mr. Beauchamp," Wall said.

The agent, who went on to lead the federal investigation of Hightower's office, was Greg Rampton. Stationed in Austin beginning in the late 1970s, Rampton launched a round of investigations into Texas state officeholders, who were all Democrats.

"I'd heard about Rampton," said Austin lawyer Buck Wood. "I was told he was a mad dog against Democrats."

Sandy-haired and bespectacled, Rampton presented an unremarkable countenance and a fierce law enforcement zeal. In 1988, two years after he had led the investigation of the bugging of Karl Rove's office, the office of Texas Land Commissioner Garry Mauro became Rampton's target.

"He showed up in my office with 18 agents," Mauro recalled. "They walked in and they had a regressive analysis. They had a list of people and this program where you could type in people who had given you contributions and you could show through regressive analysis that they had, which is very sophisticated, you were supposed to be able to show they got higher appraisals and faster turnaround times. Only problem is, they didn't. It took 'em about an hour to figure it out."

Rampton did not pull out of Mauro's office until six months later and he left the case open for two years, though there was never any proof of illegal behavior. What prompted him to take on the land commissioner's agency has never been clear, except to Mauro.

"You gotta understand, Rampton had a basic concept. Nobody gave a political contribution unless it was quid pro quo and that was against the law, so every political contribution, you give me, [Rampton] enough time and I'll prove an illegal connection."

Mauro has continued to believe that Rampton came to his office at the prompting of Karl Rove.

"You think Rove sent Rampton to your office?" he was asked.

"Oh, there's no doubt in my mind."

"You think he did?"

"No doubt in my mind. I don't think there's any doubt that he [Rampton] and Karl had lunch on a regular basis and had telephone calls on a regular basis. I think it was fairly common knowledge and they did it in public so it wasn't like they were that secretive."

Byron Sage, the special agent-in-charge of the Austin office of the FBI for 12 years, defended Rampton. He said there was never anything political about the agent's work, and if there had been, it would have not been tolerated. But assistant U.S. attorney for Austin, Dan Mills, told a lawyer for the agriculture department that he had been instructed by his superiors to "concentrate on making cases involving elected officials."

The officials were all Democrats.

Even if there is no substance to the political conspiracy theory, connections did exist for Rove to use. State auditor, Larry Alwin, who had a professed dislike of Agriculture Commissioner Jim Hightower, had ordered an audit of the ag agency. The state auditor's report was a few months away from completion when details were leaked to *Dallas Morning News* reporter Bruce Tomaso. According to staffers at the paper's Austin office, Rove was always calling with leads and ideas for stories. Though he was not the source to make first contact with Tomaso, Rove could have easily arranged for the auditor or an intermediary to get advance information of the final report of the state audit into Tomaso's hands. Eventually, Tomaso said, Rove did begin contacting him with information.

The lengthy piece included a denial from a Texas Agriculture Department spokesman who said it was just a case of Washington Republicans trying to stir up trouble for Commissioner Jim Hightower. Tomaso's listing of credit card charges, however, did look incriminating for Hightower and two of his top assistants, Deputy Agriculture Commissioner Mike Moeller, and Pete McRae. According to Tomaso's story, Hightower had spent more than $4,000 on his card in just under two years. A number of meals, exceeding $100, had been charged in Austin and Dallas, Texas; San Francisco, California; Washington, DC; Venice, California; and Fargo, North Dakota.

The general counsel for the agriculture department, Jesse Oliver, was certain the initial stories were prompted by Karl Rove to set up the Perry campaign for success.

"In terms of how it worked for him, [Rove] it boils down to him having the right contacts and he expanded his tentacles. He could gather information and use it to his candidate's benefit. He's like a rat sniffing out information all the time and piecing it back together to figure out where the food is."

Regardless of who had initiated the contact, a link had been established to reporter Tomaso. Once the first story broke, Rove had no reason to be overly cautious in leaking to Tomaso and providing him leads and tips. The controversy was now part of the public political discourse and Rove could help the journalists cover the story and still ask for source protection. He began frequent conversations with Tomaso and other Austin journalists, pointing them in directions that served his goals.

"I can't tell you for certain Karl was the only one driving that agriculture department story," David Elliot of the *Austin American-Statesman* said. "But I dealt with him a whole, whole lot, several times a week."

A few key reporters began to get leaks about subpoenas before they were even served to witnesses.

When the *Dallas Morning News* hit the Texas streets on November 13, 1989, the political problems for the agriculture department began to be compounded by legalities. The headline was, "Ag Agency Contracts Questioned." The subheading pointed out, "Beneficiary a Backer of Agricultural Official." The official was Mike Moeller, Hightower's political understudy and anointed successor to campaign for the office of agriculture commissioner. A few years earlier, Moeller supporters had formed a political action committee (PAC) called Building Texas Agriculture. While the PAC did fund general purpose interests in Texas agriculture, the eventual, unstated goal was to transition the organization and the money into the expectant candidacy of Moeller.

The chief fund-raiser and one of five board members for the Building Texas Agriculture PAC was an agency consultant. Bob Boyd, along with his associate Russell Koontz, had been involved with the Texas Department of Agriculture since the 1950s. Boyd, in particular, had been providing Hightower with a bridge to the more traditional political influences in Texas agriculture. His help, however, had gone uncompensated. With a wife at home suffering a debilitating disease, Boyd was having difficulty handling her medical bills and, therefore, decided he could no longer work for free.

"I actually engineered this thing," Pete McRae said. "He came to me and said he needed to make some money. I told Hightower we needed to do something for Bob, put him on a contract or something."

The timing for execution of the agreements could not have been worse. Boyd's deal was arranged only weeks after the PAC was formed. Boyd and Koontz also were known by both political parties to have spent years traveling the state and raising money for previous agriculture commissioners. They did their fund-raising while also serving as employees of the agency.

Boyd and Koontz intended to function as regulators and political operatives, doing their TDA business while picking up a check or two for Jim Hightower. This was the way agriculture agency business and politics had been performed for decades. The new twist to their endeavors was that they wanted to generate cash for the Building Texas Agriculture PAC because they knew, in addition to providing scholarships and promoting agriculture, it would eventually set up Mike Moeller's campaign to succeed Hightower.

Tomaso's story that November morning in 1989 said that Boyd got nearly $20,000 "while he was working to promote the political career of Deputy Agriculture Commissioner Mike Moeller." Moeller, a burly wall of a man, who came from a Texas ranching family, defended the consulting deal with Boyd.

"If he is not the most competent consultant we have ever had while I have been working here, he is very near the top. He is a personal friend of mine, no question about that. But what he does on his own time, in terms of raising money for various causes, is his own business."

By most accounts, Boyd was honest and informed donors the money might also be used to help Mike Moeller run for office after

Hightower stepped aside. Moeller's political ascension, however, had collided with Hightower's change of plans.

Hightower had decided to run for reelection, for a third term.

But his campaign was off to a bad start. And everyone on Hightower's team thought it was because of a relationship Karl Rove had with an FBI agent. Reporters, like Debbie Graves of the Austin American-Statesman, kept making calls to the agriculture agency asking about personal appearance subpoenas before the documents had ever been delivered. Hightower's staff suspected collaboration between Rove and agent Rampton. Whenever Graves called, according to former staffers, she always had the names of people who were to be subpoenaed before the individuals had even been notified.

The information being leaked to Graves could only have come from a few places. A source on a grand jury or in the U.S. attorney's office would have had the details provided Graves. But leaking it would have put at grave risk a federal investigation and the legal careers of all involved, confronting the leaker with potential federal criminal charges like obstruction of justice. The FBI and Rove were the other possible sources of leaks. Rampton would have been taking a bigger chance than Rove by getting material to reporters. Rove remains the most likely source, letting out information he may have been given by Rampton during the course of the investigation.

Appearing before the State Senate Nominations Committee several years later, Rove was questioned about a possible relationship with Rampton. Democratic State Senator Bob Glasgow submitted Rove to a series of questions. Glasgow, who lacked context and detailed familiarity with what he was asking, seemed to be trying to get Rove to admit he had schemed with FBI agent Rampton in a series of investigations of Democratic state officeholders. Rove, acutely aware of the time line of the FBI probe, almost kept things straight, until he began talking about his work in Rick Perry's campaign.

"I do know that I became involved in the campaign of Rick Perry in November of 1989. At that point, there was already an FBI investigation ongoing of the Texas Department of Agriculture, prompted by stories, which had appeared in August and September, I believe, in the *Dallas Morning News* regarding the use of Department of Agriculture funds."

Rove's answer ruins his credibility. If he was, indeed, aware of the ongoing FBI probe of Hightower in November 1989, he knew about it a month before the Department of Agriculture had been informed by subpoena. Moreover, Rove's assumption that the newspaper stories prompted the investigation was just that, an assumption—unless he knew it directly from the FBI.

Rove's descriptions of his encounters with Greg Rampton have varied through the years. There is no doubt the agent and the consultant interacted but how much is unclear. Before the Nominations Committee, Rove's answers appeared inconsistent and almost Clintonesque when he was asked about Rampton.

"How long have you known an FBI agent by the name of Greg Rampton?" Senator Glasgow asked.

"Ah, Senator, it depends. Would you define know for me?"

"What is your relationship with him?"

"Ah, I know, I would not recognize Greg [Rampton] if he walked in the door. We have talked on the phone a var . . . a number of times. Ah, and he has visited in my office once or twice. But we do not have a social or personal relationship whatsoever."

As unremarkable as Rampton might have been as a physical presence, it also was difficult to believe that the agent had been in Rove's office for a conversation, and now, less than a year later, Rove would not be able to identify him. One gift Rove possesses is a keen memory, so good he regularly recalled the most minute details of history or the exact date he contemplated taking a picture off his office wall.

Interviewed during his White House years about a possible relationship with Rampton, Rove made it sound as if there was never more than a solitary phone conversation between himself and the agent.

"I don't recall whether I called Rampton or he called me. I have a vague recollection that he called me to say, if you know of anything, let us know."

Frequently, Rove has appeared to exhibit selective recall. His political memory is legendary. In the same interview where Rove suggested there was nothing more than a phone call, he later considered the possibility he may have met with Rampton.

"I can't remember if it was a meeting or a phone call. I met him somewhere, along the way, but I can't remember. The whole idea that I had control over the FBI . . ."

At least once, Karl Rove did meet with FBI agent Rampton, and he remembered it. In 1990, President George H. W. Bush nominated Rove to the Board for International Broadcasting and he had to fill out a sworn document for the Senate Committee on Foreign Relations. Under Part E of the questionnaire, identified as Ethical Matters, question number five asked, "Have you been interviewed or asked to supply any information in connection with any administrative or grand jury investigation in the past eighteen months?"

The answer was the first definitive proof that Rove had, in fact, consulted with FBI agent Rampton, and from a strictly technical perspective, it contradicted his sworn testimony to the Texas Senate.

"This summer [1990] I met with agent Greg Rampton of the Austin FBI office at his request regarding a probe of political corruption in the office of Texas Agriculture Commissioner Jim Hightower."

Whether Rove's information launched the investigation or he simply ended up assisting an eager FBI agent will likely never be known.

The FBI, though, had not yet formally begun its probe in November 1989, and Pete McRae was already worried. He knew how bad things looked to the average newspaper reader. He was troubled over how Karl Rove was likely to use information in the newspaper stories. And just as concerned by what Rove did not yet know and what he might do when he learned it.

Whatever Pete McRae and Mike Moeller were thinking, they still had to have been cheered by the release of the state auditor's report. While charging that their agency had been run with "an absence of effective control," the December 1, 1989, summary, according to

Auditor Larry Alwin, "generally corroborated" the agriculture department's claims it was doing nothing improper.

The day the report was issued there was a celebration in the executive offices of the Texas Department of Agriculture. Hightower, Moeller, and McRae all had reason to be pleased with the outcome. First, USDA had cleared them with "no provable violations of federal law" and now the Texas state auditor had carefully checked their operations and had found nothing improper.

"We were drinking a beer and just cackling," Pete McRae recalled. "Jesse [Oliver, TDA legal counsel] said, 'You know, we really ought to let these guys win one of these things, once in a while.' We had won every issue over the last couple of years."

They thought they had kicked down Republican schemes to harm Hightower and the agriculture department.

"That was the pivotal thought," Jesse Oliver said, "that we had won, beat them on the issues, and now they had to go back and lick their wounds. We didn't know that they wouldn't quit. We just didn't realize that whoever was doing this thing would come back again and again to come after us."

But they were coming. And Karl Rove wasn't just one of them. He was their general, the battle tactician and leader.

And he didn't like to lose.

5

Running for Cover

Tricks and treachery are the practice of fools that don't have brains enough to be honest.

—Benjamin Franklin

The story of the auditor's report of the Texas Department of Agriculture had barely cleared the front pages of Texas newspapers when State Representative Rick Perry announced he was a Republican candidate for agriculture commissioner. Two months earlier, Perry had abandoned his Democratic background and switched to the GOP during a high profile news conference. Before talking with reporters about his campaign against Jim Hightower, Perry had told a rural newspaper that Kenneth Boatwright, his opposition in the primary, was planning to withdraw and support him.

Hightower's campaign staff searched in vain for Karl Rove's fingerprints on Boatwright's decision to quit. Rove acknowledged in a 2002 interview that he had met with Boatwright but insisted he had no involvement in the former agriculture department worker's political plans.

During his session with reporters, Rick Perry also implied that he knew more problems were ahead for Hightower. Even though the USDA and the Texas state auditor had refuted allegations of illegalities by Hightower, Perry said, "USDA officials are not through looking at those expenditures yet, and I think we've just seen the tip of the iceberg on those expenditures."

How could Perry have known? Was Karl Rove speaking with the FBI and telling Perry what he was learning from the investigation?

Perry's pronouncement used the same phrase as Boatwright when he issued a news release about his own candidacy. It made Hightower's staff think Rove had written the statements for both men.

Hightower had scheduled his own announcement for reelection at a farm rally in the panhandle town of Dawn, Texas, for two weeks after Perry's event, December 18.

FBI agent Greg Rampton also had plans for December 18, 1989.

Unannounced, Rampton arrived at the offices of the Texas Department of Agriculture and asked to see Hightower. He was not in the office. Instead of delivering it to Hightower, the agent handed a federal grand jury subpoena to an aide. The document requested contract and personnel records on consultant Bob Boyd.

Hightower's team immediately suspected Karl Rove's involvement, especially since the Rampton visit was the same day as Hightower's scheduled announcement. They believed the delivery of the federal court subpoenas were timed for political effect, to cover up news of Hightower's announcement.

"I do know he played a role in it," Mike Moeller said. "I don't think there's any question about that. And I think Rampton was willing to let him play a role. I think he wanted to know what Rampton was hearing, in some cases, before Rampton heard it. They shared information."

Things were not the way they appeared, according to Rove. His client, Rick Perry, Rove said, was just a lucky guy, Rove recalled in 2002.

"I will just tell you this, the Rick Perry campaign for ag commissioner, the myth has grown into the manipulation of the world intelligence, total conspiracy theory. This is the world's most fortuitous human being. Talk about being in the right place at the right time."

Maybe. But somebody was talking to reporters.

By January 12, the first reporter's inquiry on the investigation came from Debbie Graves of the Austin American-Statesman. Graves contacted the press office of the Texas Department of Agriculture (TDA) wanting to know about rumors of an FBI investigation. She had the names of people who were to be subpoenaed.

"Debbie Graves had inside knowledge about the first personal appearance subpoenas," Pete McRae said. "She called and asked to talk to specific people at the ag department who had gotten them. Only trouble was, they hadn't gotten them yet. She called days before they were even delivered."

Although nothing had been publicly released about a federal probe, reporters seemed to know where to look for information and what to ask for. On the same day that Graves called the ag department, January 24, the Texas comptroller's office received open records requests from the *Austin American-Statesman* and the *Dallas Morning News*. Both papers were fishing in the same pond. They wanted payment documents and relevant materials related to Bob Boyd. Who steered them there and told them to ask about Bob Boyd? Was it Rampton or Rove or someone inside the grand jury?

Agent Rampton had already asked for the same records. He spent February 1990 expanding his investigation while publicity about it was also on the increase. Rampton informed numerous people inside and out of the Texas Department of Agriculture he wanted to interview them. The questions were all characterized by an attempt to acquire information on work performed by Bob Boyd and Russell Koontz and any records of how they were compensated. During these interviews, Rampton made it abundantly clear he thought the two men were not doing any work under their consulting agreements and had spent their days raising money for Hightower, the Building Texas Agriculture political action committee (PAC), and Mike Moeller.

The story of the investigation, which first broke in the newspapers, followed Rampton and Rove's theme. The *Dallas Morning News* Austin bureau correspondent Christy Hoppe interviewed Commissioner Hightower about $6600 he had received in campaign contributions. According to her sources, Boyd solicited the money while he was on agriculture department business. Financial disclosure reports from the Hightower campaign showed that the donations came a day after the visits by Boyd.

Mike Moeller read the article and was incensed. As if TDA did not have enough troubles with stories about credit card usage and now they were giving ammunition to Karl Rove and Republican Rick Perry. The deputy agriculture commissioner expected to get hammered even harder by these latest allegations concerning the behavior of Boyd.

And that's what happened.

Rick Perry, who was under the managerial guidance of Karl Rove, began making even greater use of the investigation as an issue. Perry's campaign put out a statement saying, "The problems at TDA are spreading like the fire ant problem. In both cases, the commissioner has done little to squelch the spread."

Mike Moeller just wanted to make sure there was no further damage.

"I am the one who called in Boyd and Koontz and said, 'What in the hell is going on?' I told them to stop it and stop it now. That turned out to be the end of it. It did stop."

The negative stories in the newspaper, however, did not stop.

Thursday morning's paper in Austin, the day after Christy Hoppe's story was published in the *Dallas Morning News*, carried a huge banner headline across the top of the front page: *Hightower Consultant Investigated.* Debbie Graves, the reporter who had made several calls to the agriculture department asking about unconfirmed reports of an FBI investigation, wrote that a federal grand jury was looking into misuse of public funds. Graves said that unnamed sources had confirmed the U.S. government was trying to determine if consultant Bob Boyd had been paid to raise campaign funds for Commissioner Jim Hightower and the prospective race of Mike Moeller, before Hightower had decided to seek a third term.

Reporters were consistently getting information about the investigation before the agriculture department and the individuals being investigated. Additionally, employees of the agriculture department were being solicited to provide insider information. According to Moeller, numerous agency workers were approached and told that, if they had allegations to make, they should take them to Karl Rove. Rove was accused of screening employees' stories and deciding which ones were to be taken to the FBI.

Agriculture agency officials also thought Rove was behind the leaks and was working with an old Republican ally, the Texas Farm Bureau.

Vernie R. Glasson, executive director of the Texas Farm Bureau, wrote to the organization's national director in Washington, DC, on February 7, 1990, exactly one week before Hoppe's piece in the Dallas paper. In his letter to John C. Datt, Glasson wrote, "What we need is some kind of full-scale (or otherwise) investigation into State/Federal relationships between USDA and the Texas Department of Agriculture."

The text of his letter indicated that Glasson had been tipped by somebody that the FBI was already hard at work talking to TDA employees.

"I understand there might be some kind of investigation underway. What would help is a February 15 or so (prior to March 13) announcement, or leak to Texas Press (particularly, the *Dallas Morning News*). We are confident there are many skeletons in the closet and they need to be rattled."

Making something happen before March 13 was important because that was the day of the Texas Democratic Primary. Attorneys for the TDA cited the letter as proof that Karl Rove's tentacles were reaching across the state and deploying his operatives. The letter, in some respects, is what Texas political operatives describe as "classic Rove." If there are enough institutions and people involved in an effort to discredit and leak, there is no way to pin the blame on him. If nothing else, the Farm Bureau letter's date is proof that someone had informed the organization of an FBI investigation long before the public had been made aware of any probe.

One week after Glasson suggested a leak, Hoppe's story showed up in the Dallas paper. And in conversations with attorneys for some of the agriculture agency staffers, FBI agent Greg Rampton said he had become aware of "sham contracts." According to numerous agriculture department workers, Rampton threatened obstruction of justice charges against people because they were all hiring lawyers before agreeing to FBI interviews. Before the investigation had concluded, many employees of the agriculture department had accused agent Rampton of questionable tactics. Several said they were accused of perjury, tampering with evidence, and obstruction of justice, often just for demanding they be allowed to have an attorney present when questioned.

Special agent-in-charge of the bureau's Austin office, Byron Sage, said he thought interview subjects simply misinterpreted Rampton.

"There are a lot of different ways to conduct an interview. I can see where someone might feel threatened. But I'm certain Greg never did anything to openly intimidate people. It just was not his style. This guy was one of the best investigators around and was strictly by the book. And I worked with a lot of good ones during my time with the bureau."

Rampton has spoken about his role in the agriculture department investigation on only two occasions. Mary Lenz of the Houston Post was able to get Rampton on the phone and asked him if he thought he was being used to play partisan politics and discredit Democrats.

"That's like saying, 'When did you stop beating your wife?'" he told Lenz. "I can say that never entered the picture at all."

Years after the investigation of Hightower's office had concluded, columnist Molly Ivins spoke with the agent about consistent
allegations from Hightower and Democrats that Rampton was col-
laborating and sharing information with GOP operative Karl Rove.

"Let me think. I couldn't recall talking to him on that particular
case at all. If there was a conversation we had on that case, I can't recall it. He was not an integral part of that case. I don't even remember bouncing anything off of him as somebody who was familiar
with politics in Austin."

The quote meant that either Rampton or Rove was confused,
had a bad memory, or was simply lying, because in Rove's sworn
statement to the Board for International Broadcasting, Rove said he
"met" with Rampton. Also, in his testimony before the Texas Senate
Nominations Committee, Rove conceded that he had talked with
Rampton a few times, possibly in person.

The apparent contradictions may not mean anything more than
the fact that political attacks are always hard to prove. The federal
investigation of Texas Department of Agriculture fell off the pages
of state newspapers until September, in the heat of the election campaign, when FBI agent Greg Rampton turned up at the secretary
of state's office. Signing his name and affiliation on the office register, Rampton asked for copies of campaign contribution reports for
Hightower and Democrat Bob Bullock, the state comptroller who
was running for lieutenant governor. It was inevitable that reporters,
who were constantly checking with the secretary of state on campaign funding issues, would see Rampton's name and find out that he
had copied finance statements for the two Democrats.

Bullock called it a "gut job."

"Nixonian dirty tricks," Hightower charged. "They've caught us
with our pants up. He [Rampton] didn't want those campaign reports. He wants the headlines."

In spite of all he had done prior to visiting the secretary of state's
office, that singular public act increased agent Rampton's profile and
caused intense scrutiny of the FBI's endeavors. Some of the state's

newspapers began to editorialize in Hightower's favor. But it was not sufficient to save his political career.

Republican Rick Perry upset Hightower by about 50,000 votes.

Perry, who became the governor of Texas when George W. Bush was elected president, passed off the glory to his consultant, Karl Rove.

"He did everything. He says, 'Here's who to hire. Here's who not to hire. Here's how to run the campaign.' He showed me a plan and pointed to it. Lots of numbers. He points to it. He says, 'You'll stay pretty much underground until this point.'"

Not surprisingly, the defeated Hightower campaign also credited Rove. Pete McRae has cemented his belief that Rove did not just make Perry a viable candidate, but also was closely involved with the federal investigation and FBI agent Rampton.

"I'm one hundred percent convinced. My experience is in Texas politics and how it works and what the stakes are. Rick Perry could not have won that initial race in '90 against Hightower without hitting a home run ball. It was Karl's job to make sure that happened."

While Hightower lost the political election, he escaped the federal probe. None of the agriculture department staffers was willing to cooperate with agent Rampton and give him evidence, possibly implicating Hightower.

And they paid for their loyalty.

On January 8, 1991, only days before Rick Perry was sworn in as the new Texas agriculture commissioner, federal indictments were returned against Deputy Agriculture Commissioner Mike Moeller, administrator Pete McRae, executive director Bill Quicksall, and agriculture department consultants Bob Boyd and Russell Koontz.

Taking office after the indictments became public; Perry hired an ethics advisor to help the agriculture department undo any damage incurred by the federal investigation. The man he named to the job was Larry Beauchamp, the investigator for the district attorney who had also worked for Perry's brother-in-law. Beauchamp's request of USDA records, and his subsequent admission that it was "possible" he turned them over to the FBI, may have been what prompted the federal probe.

The next summer, Tom Smith, executive director of the government watchdog group Texas Public Citizen, was asked by the Austin paper to comment on Beauchamp's tactics and his relationship to Perry.

"This begins to appear as if there was a concerted effort to influence the outcome of an election by starting investigations and rumors. This is one of the oldest tricks in the 'How to Win an Election Handbook.' It is beyond belief that all of these events are coincidental," Smith said.

Contacted in 2002, Beauchamp refused to talk about any possible involvement in the investigation of TDA. "I don't talk to the media," he said. "And I don't want to be in any book."

The closest Karl Rove ever came to acknowledging the possibility of his own involvement or the Perry campaign's was during brief comments to John Gravois of the *Houston Post*'s Austin bureau. Rove conceded it was "conceivable" someone in the campaign may have been feeding allegations and information to the FBI, but he was not guilty of the tactic, he insisted. Anyone who did such a thing, Rove claimed, did it independently and there was no campaign official involved.

Regardless of his claims to the contrary, there is no plausible way Karl Rove did not take part in the federal investigation of the Texas Department of Agriculture. His sworn statement that he met with FBI agent Greg Rampton is an indication of likely participation. If the federal agent was conducting an unbiased probe into the Texas Department of Agriculture, why did he need to speak with the political operative trying to unseat the Democratic office holder? At a minimum, Rove and Rampton being together has the appearance of impropriety and unfairness. And his several versions of denial have never sounded true. Of course, there was no reason for Rove to decline to take part in Rampton's work.

He had much to gain by helping out. And he gained it: further political influence and power as he cleared Texas of Democratic officeholders and transformed the state into an emerging Republican stronghold. By the time a federal trial had concluded two years later, Mike Moeller and Pete McRae were each sentenced to 27 months in federal prison. Democratic Agriculture Commissioner Jim Hightower, Rove, and agent Rampton's obvious target, escaped prosecution.

"Moeller and McRae didn't do anything different than what happens in Texas politics about, oh, only a thousand times a day," said Glenn Smith, a Democratic political consultant.

Their sentences were handed down on Friday, November 19, 1993.

Karl Rove was busily preparing George W. Bush's first run for governor of Texas.

D efense attorney Gerry Spence had reached a critical moment in the Ruby Ridge trial. In 30 years of criminal defense, the famed Wyoming lawyer had not lost a case. And he was not going to have this nationally prominent prosecution be the first time he failed.

Spence was defending Randy Weaver, whose wife and son had been shot by federal agents when they tried to arrest him at his mountain cabin. Weaver and a friend had been charged with killing a deputy marshal while resisting arrest.

Some of the government's evidence had bothered Spence. In particular, he could not figure why one bullet casing from the scene had appeared so pristine. The shell came from a Ruger Mini-14 and Spence had dubbed it "the magic bullet." He was convinced an FBI agent, or someone else trying to protect the government's sharpshooters from prosecution, had planted it there. When he suggested his theory, the FBI said it was impossible.

A few days earlier, Spence had called to the stand Special Agent Greg Rampton of the Boise, Idaho, office of the FBI and had questioned him about a series of photographs, which the agency had admitted into evidence. Rampton was called back to the witness stand after the U.S. attorney informed the court that some of the evidence in a few of the photos from the crime scene had been staged.

Spence was about to prove the FBI was manufacturing evidence.

"You knew before the trial that the pictures I had were reconstructed when I cross-examined you the other day, isn't that true?" he asked Rampton.

"You never asked me about that and I tried to stick with the questions you asked me," Rampton replied.

After Rampton's admission that the FBI had doctored evidence, there was little else Spence had to do to make sure his client was acquitted.

One of Rampton's colleagues in the bureau told the government prosecutor before the trial began, two months earlier, that the photos were re-creations of the crime scene. The pictures did not show the evidence where the FBI found it, according the government's own lawyer. The government had screwed up. Shell casings were removed too quickly. Agents replaced them and then "reshot" photos of the evidence.

The prosecutor had not informed the court of that fact until the trial was nearing conclusion. Rampton's testimony meant the government's case against separatist Randy Weaver had no possibility of winning a conviction.

Agent Rampton had been transferred to Boise, Idaho, after concluding an investigation involving agriculture department employees in Texas. Democrats said the FBI agent had been relocated because they had built a convincing case against Rampton that he was persecuting Democrats, cooperating with Republican operatives like Karl Rove, and leaking information about personal appearance subpoenas to reporters before the documents had ever been delivered.

"That's a bunch of crap," said Byron Sage, former special agent-in-charge of the Austin office of the FBI. "Greg did a great job in Austin. He and his wife wanted to get their kids back closer to family in Salt Lake City. They were Mormons. He wanted to go to Boise, and let me just tell you, if you've done something wrong at the bureau, you don't get transferred to the place you've requested."

At Ruby Ridge, Rampton admitted on the stand that the FBI, in a case where he was a key agent, was involved with what he had once accused employees of the Texas Department of Agriculture of doing; tampering with evidence and obstructing justice. No one in the FBI, however, was charged or tried.

"These are phony and reconstructed photos we've had in our possession the whole time," Spence told the jury.

After Rampton's testimony, Spence was so confident the government had failed to prove its case he did not even bother to present a defense.

The jury acquitted Randy Weaver.

None of this had any effect on Greg Rampton's career. He was transferred again, this time to Denver, where he rose to special agent-in-charge of the Denver office.

During his tenure in Colorado, Rampton led the FBI's Y2k project to seek out millennialist groups and domestic terrorists. When gun rights activists and conservatives claimed the government's Project Megiddo was making a move on their constitutional rights, Rampton went on a radio talk show to defend the bureau and calm down critics.

The agent was poised, handling adversarial calls with the polish of a seasoned political candidate.

"I think that there's, in general, a healthy skepticism about anything the government does; and, unfortunately, that can sometimes hinder the truth. A wise man once said, 'Truth is always in short supply, but invariably supply exceeds demand.' So I think we have to be very careful about our skepticism, and, hopefully, that it will lead us to the truth, and not away from the truth."

FBI agent Greg Rampton retired from the Denver office of the bureau as a special agent-in-charge.

If anyone in the taxpaying public calls the Denver office to inquire of Rampton's whereabouts, they are informed he left no forwarding address.

6

Proof of Performance

Whether you think you can or think you can't—you are right.
—Henry Ford

The plane cut a straight line across the winter sky. After leveling out at 35,000 feet, the Gulfstream was already moving over the dark bottomland of the upper Mississippi valley. All of the Bush campaign staff onboard had reason to be optimistic. A few, undoubtedly, were staring out the window at the brittle February landscape of Iowa and Illinois. Atop the jet stream, the aircraft slipped easily eastward toward Manchester, New Hampshire. Before the landing gear squawked across the runway in New England, the Bush team had completed the psychological transition from dreamers to believers. This, they had begun to realize, could actually happen.

Iowa was behind them, in the dark; victory only hours old. Texas Governor George W. Bush had just won his initial test in the race for the Republican nomination for president. He would be back for another try in four more years but winning the nomination was the first goal. Reelection was little more than a theoretical concept. Knowing the news value of the present moment, however, Bush and a key advisor, Karen Hughes, had invited a select group of writers to join them on the candidate's private jet. Taking seats in a lounge area at the back of the plane, Frank Bruni of the *New York Times*, Judy Keene of *USA Today*, Glenn Johnson with the Associated Press, and Wayne Slater from the *Dallas Morning News*, were strapped in for the quick run to the northeast. The governor was hoping to attend an indoor rally at 3:00 A.M. in a Manchester airport hangar, celebrating his Iowa win.

Uncharacteristically, Karl Rove, a man in constant motion, appeared to be dozing at the front of the aircraft. Lying in the leather seat of the Gulfstream, eyes closed, his legs were stretched out before him. Rove seemed almost serene, not at all the kinetic, combustible force that had confronted reporter Wayne Slater two months earlier on the tarmac in Manchester. There was no longer any reason for him to be jittery about the campaign's prospects in the Iowa caucuses. Bush had won. After two years of preparation, building a financial network, courting the party elite, cultivating a mounting presence in the media, creating the persona of front-runner, after years of meticulous groundwork, Team Bush had finally won its first official victory of the 2000 presidential campaign. Rove had delivered, as promised.

Out the window, a circle of moon hung just above the wing. It was past midnight in the heartland. In two weeks, the cranky, independent-minded voters of New Hampshire were to hand the governor his head in the primary, the big test in his quest for the presidency. In the afterglow of Iowa, though, Bush was jazzed, lumbering through the tiny cabin with an adolescent exuberance, belying the grim future that awaited him and America in the aftermath of 9/11. Inexplicably, Bush was wearing plastic ski shades and orange ear plugs, feeling his way along, identifying people by touching faces and heads.

"Logan," he announced, delighted by his correct identification of travel aide Logan Walters. Then, laying hands on someone else, he assumed the caricature of a tent-show preacher.

"Heal!" he declared.

The adrenaline was pumping, and Bush was relieved and excited that he had bested the Republican field. The GOP front-runner for more than a year, he had been catapulted to the lead by his name and a mountain of campaign cash. It was not until Iowa, though, that he had actually won an election, the first event of the presidential season. His father had finished second in Iowa in 1988, but he had won the nomination. In the warm glow of the jet, with his wife sleeping nearby and his most loyal aides around him, Bush allowed himself to think, for one forbidden, delicious, rogue moment, of the end game in which he was to retake the White House for the Bush family.

"This was a big moment today," he told the four reporters. "It'll be eclipsed by the next big moment, then the next big moment, leading up to the biggest of all moments."

Sitting among the journalists in the rear of the plane, Bush was momentarily pensive. Wayne Slater reminded the governor there was a long road ahead.

"What if you lose?" Slater wondered aloud.

Bush's face grew solemn, thinking about his father, who had won the White House only to be turned out for a second term.

"I won't like it. I've seen a great man lose more than once. I know full well life goes on, but I don't want to lose. I don't think I will lose."

In the window of the jet, lights speckled the broad farmland below. Bush turned back to the reporters after gazing at the fleeing dark.

"Sometimes, there are forces greater in the process, things that are totally out of my control. I don't know what they will be. But I know so far we're running a campaign that, if there's a chance, we'll win. This is a very well run campaign, a great team. The strategy seems to be working."

Adjacent to him, eyes closed, sat the man responsible for that strategy. Smiling, Karl Rove's thin hair was tangled in disarray, his shirt disheveled. Stuck to his forehead and braced by his glasses was a card he'd pick up from somewhere. It bore the word "Press," one of the many forces to be managed along the way to victory.

"Fabulous," he said, a favorite word in the Rove lexicon when things were going well.

More than anyone, Karl Rove had gotten Bush to this point, and everyone knew it. He was the genius of the campaign, the tactician, and the guru. Everyone described him as brainy, the brainy Karl Rove, who spouted voter statistics and arcane political data like a geyser. When he had arrived in Texas to set up shop, there were no statewide Republican officeholders. Twenty years later, Republicans sat in every state office from governor through Supreme Court, and most had been Rove clients.

In George W. Bush, though, lay the instrument of a larger plan. Rove had worked for the father at the Republican National Committee in Washington, where he first met the son. Later, in Texas, he became chief political advisor to the younger Bush, preparing him to run for governor, steering the politics of his administration and developing the blueprint to win the White House. In Bush, Rove had seen the perfect vehicle for his ambitions to become the single most influential political figure in Washington.

"To Karl, the man with the plan," Bush had written on a photo that hung in Rove's office years before the presidential race.

They were complimentary figures, Bush and Rove, each offering elements the other lacked. Rove was cerebral; Bush never liked going too deeply into the homework. Rove had an encyclopedic mind and a gift for campaign arithmetic; Bush had engaging people skills, a knack for winning over opponents with pure charm. If Rove approached politics as a blood sport, Bush's instinct was to search out compromise and agreement. They offered each other a perfect counterbalance.

They also shared some important traits. Though they came from different academic backgrounds, Bush was the product of Yale; Rove never graduated from college, each harbored a deep suspicion of the gratuitous intellectualism of the Ivy League. Bush saw in Rove extreme loyalty, which the family valued above all other things. In Bush, Rove saw an aspect of his own personality, a relentless focus and self-discipline. This man could be president, Rove concluded early on.

Rove may have already realized, in this odd place, seven miles in the sky over America, he was slumbering in the seat adjacent to the next president of the United States. The road was long and getting longer. Still, he had directed the governor's race, helped develop the agenda, managed the policies of the Bush administration, and cleared every political appointment. He had been the architect of Bush's reelection, organizer of the early presidential money machine, and tactical genius behind a political field operation that was to deliver the Republican nomination for president. Along the way, he had damaged the reputations of political enemies and assisted the fortunes of friends, and understood, probably down to a cellular level, that his dream was unfolding perfectly.

"Bush is the kind of candidate and officeholder political hacks like me wait a lifetime to be associated with," he told a reporter.

Ahead lay victory and the White House. From the moment the Bush team moved into the West Wing, Karl Rove extended his considerable influence over the affairs of the office. Taxes, tariffs, the Middle East. Nothing was able to escape his political prism. Congressional leaders, corporate America, political consultants, journalists, and all people of influence came seeking Rove's advice and guidance. The man with the plan, in the end, did not only affect the affairs of political Washington, but also the lives of every American.

"Fabulous," Rove said, extending his legs further. "Fabuloso."

They were well into the race and the campaign was clicking for Rove and his candidate. Sure, there were some things out there yet that might cause him or the governor some problems. But reporters weren't asking. So, he wasn't telling. Besides, nobody had any proof that Karl Rove had done anything in Texas, except run winning campaigns. And all of the tactics he deployed in Texas, the things he had learned from those campaigns, Rove intended to deploy in the biggest contest of all: the race for president of the United States.

7

The Boy Who Forgot to Be a Boy

There is always one moment in childhood when the door opens
and lets the future in.

—Graham Greene

Karl Rove moved through the hallways of Olympus High in
the late 1960s like a thunderstorm, full of noise and elec-
tricity. He was going in all directions at once, pieces of
motion, everything flung out in all directions, arms,
hands, mouth—mostly his mouth, which moved in an avalanche of
words. Rove was always talking. He had opinions on everything,
which he shared generously: on McNamara's prosecution of the
Vietnam War, on defects in New Deal liberalism, on food in the
cafeteria and the class schedule, on deoxyribonucleic acid, and military conscription, and an inevitable cure for the common cold. He
had an opinion on every subject, every day, and on this day the subject was Karl Rove, candidate for president of the student senate at
Olympus School, Salt Lake City, Utah.

He passed through the halls, reviewing the campaign posters,
both his and those of his opponent, John Sorensen. Sorensen was
junior class president, one of the Mormon kids, smart and popular

and confident of victory. Rove was an ace debater who carried into the arena of high school a spindly body in Hush Puppies and horn rims. There was never a day, classmates remember, that Rove did not wear a coat and tie. He was, by his own account, a "big nerd, complete with the pocket protector, briefcase, the whole deal." At the same time, there was something oddly compelling about him, friends remember. He had a kind of energized personality that transcended, even then, his nerdy nature.

Classmate Rick Higgins considered Rove completely confident.

"He never doubted where he stood. He established his position and, by god, that's where it was. Karl had enormous focus, he just zeroed in and was extremely tenacious."

He was also bright, scary bright.

"He was so smart and so able to communicate with people that he was like a magnet," recalled classmate Glenn Hargreaves.

The student senate was the governing council for the student body. It organized student forums, arranged assemblies, debated school issues, and passed resolutions to improve things at Olympus High. About two dozen students made up the senate, representing homerooms and school organizations. The president, elected by the student body, set the agenda and presided over the meetings. In other words, the president of the senate was at the heart of every issue on campus. This was politics and Karl Rove loved politics.

When the day came for the assembly where candidates were to formally present themselves, Rove was ready. He had analyzed what it would take to win—three parts preparation, one part surprise— and had put a plan in effect. He was always the man with the plan.

"He was task-oriented," recalled Rick Higgins, a high school classmate.

"It didn't matter how much it took to become prepared, he was better prepared than anyone else. That was the goal. That's what he did."

Rove had recruited a core of supporters and plastered the walls with posters. He had methodically pursued student support, in the hallways, in classrooms, at the long rows of lunch tables in the cafeteria. He pitched himself furiously, promising great things. It was hilarious how serious he was about a school election.

Sorenson, Rove's opponent in the race, understood more clearly in hindsight.

"You have to remember high school is basically a popularity contest. Karl is extremely bright. He was on the debate team, could basically debate anything and win any argument. He could debate that the sky was black when it was blue and he could debate it was blue when it was black. And he would succeed."

As for Sorensen, he was the candidate of experience, the junior class president. He was rail-thin with a thatch of blond hair and a ready smile—the perfect candidate. Those running for office tried to do something to catch people's attention and prompt them to vote for you.

Sorensen decided to make a play on his name.

His name was John so he pulled a mock outhouse into the hall. Wrapping up his campaign appeal, Sorensen turned and pretended to flush, and to the sound of a flushing toilet and the rising chant—Vote for John! Vote for John!—he walked triumphantly around the gym floor, toilet paper dangling from his pants, and accepted the cheers of the crowd.

"Everybody went crazy," he said. "I thought, hey, I've got this in the bag."

Walking off the floor, though, Sorensen noticed something odd. Someone had removed the doors to the shop, to create a wider entrance to the gym. Outside, although he couldn't see it at this moment, was his opponent, preparing for entry. Years later, in a political memo that launched the Republican takeover of Texas, Rove outlined for a political candidate what it takes to win. He quoted Napoleon: "The whole art of war consists in a well-reasoned and extremely circumspect defensive, followed by rapid and audacious attack."

That's what he was doing in a high school contest.

Suddenly, into the gymnasium came Karl Rove in the back of a Volkswagen convertible, a pretty girl on each side. He was sitting up on the back seat in coat and tie, waving his arms broadly like a candidate in a parade. The car wheeled around the gym floor. He was both the candidate and someone mocking the conventions of candidacy. He waved wildly, grinning, thin and eeky, his eyes blazing with delight behind enormous horn-rim glasses. The place erupted.

Sorenson understood, in that moment, he was not going to be elected.

"Well, obviously, you could tell who was going to win. I knew I had lost."

In everything, Karl Rove always wanted to win. He was a gyroscope, spinning around on a single point, and that point was politics. When he was 9, he chose sides in the presidential race between John Kennedy and Richard Nixon. He chose Nixon.

"The little girl across the street I can remember beating the hell out of me in 1960 because I was for Nixon and she was for Kennedy. She had a couple of years and a few pounds on me, and I can remember being on the pavement," Rove later told a reporter for the New York Times.

His sister, Reba Hammond, said Karl was consumed by politics at an early age. While other kids had posters of rock stars or sports figures on their walls, he had a poster above his bed that said, "Wake up, America."

Reba said politics enthralled him. "He was always going to be president."

Growing up, Rove's family moved around a lot. His father, Louis, was a mineral geologist and was away from home much of the time working. The household was not particularly happy. Louis and Reba Wood Rove argued, and by the time Karl had finished high school, his parents had split. The family—two sisters, three brothers—had moved from Nevada to Salt Lake City just as Karl was entering high school.

Salt Lake City was not where he was first introduced to politics, but it was the place that incubated his obsession and Republican politics in particular. The conservative city sat on a landscape dominated by two monuments—the copper dome of the state capitol and the spires of the Mormon Church. God and church and state. There was no easy way to determine where one stopped and other began. The church was the dominant religious, political, and social force in Utah and divided the community into two camps: the majority who were Mormons and the minority who were not.

Every day at Olympus High, the Mormon kids trooped across the street to the Latter Day Saints seminary for a class in religious instruction. The Mormon Church built seminaries near public schools so students would choose seminary as an elective. Once a day, the Mormon students stepped off campus for seminary, while Rove and the rest—the Mormon kids called them the gentiles—stayed behind. He spent a lot of time in the library, reading and building a prodigious set of debate cards.

Very early at Olympus High, Rove knew he wanted to be part of the debate team. Debate was a perfect melding of two things—words and opinions—and he had plenty of both. The star of the debate team his sophomore year was a senior named Keith Roark, who became a lawyer and ran unsuccessfully in 2002 for attorney general in Idaho, as a Democrat.

Roark was president of the debate club and captain of the debate team. He seemed to be everything Rove was not—at least not yet—confident, self-possessed, and physically impressive.

Rove latched onto him immediately.

"I didn't think of him as a great debater at that point in time. He was a little guy, diminutive with glasses half as big as his head. A classic towhead. He had a very high, irritating voice and something of an immature manner. But it was pretty clear he was focused. What struck me then, and still strikes me now, was the fact that when I first met him, he was a dyed-in-the-wool Republican. It was somewhat peculiar, even in conservative Salt Lake City, for anyone of his age to be so deeply interested in politics."

Roark noticed something else, too. Rove was obsessively well prepared.

"His card file was twice the size of anybody else's."

Debaters kept their arguments on 3 × 5 cards, which they carried about in shoeboxes or metal containers. Rove had the most impressive collection of debate cards at Olympus High. If his teammates had a shoebox filled with cards, Rove carried two, which he plunked down on the table in an ominous display of force.

By his senior year, the arsenal had swelled to 5 or 10 boxes. Rove figured that if two or three boxes unnerved an opposing team, why not something truly overwhelming? Why not a table full of cards? Why not buy them by the thousands and wheel them in on hand-carts? Why not throw the fear of God into the enemy before the debate even began?

The thing was, the thing nobody knew was, that the cards were mostly fake.

"We went out and bought thousands, if not tens of thousands, of debate cards," said debate partner Emil Langeland, now a lawyer in Salt Lake City.

"Everybody was using 3 by 5 debate cards. And we decided we'd better have 4 by 6—a little bigger than the next guy. And we had shoeboxes, a table full. We would come in and set up those boxes with file cards in them, color-coded, with tabs sticking up, and there were literally thousands and thousands of them. And you know what? There wasn't a thing on 99 percent of them.

"If they gave us a 4 by 4 table, we'd make it a 4 by 8 table and we'd stack this information—what appeared to be information—on the table. We'd lay out all these papers. The reality was that the core of our attack or strategy was on 20 or 30 cards. We never used much more than that. But we'd just hand truck them in, then go back out into the hall and hand truck another set in and set them up on the table almost to the point where you couldn't see us. It was all psychological, to psych out your opponent."

Rove didn't just want to win; he wanted the opponents destroyed. His worldview was clear even then: There was his team and the other team, and he would make the other team pay. He would defeat them, slaughter them, and humiliate them. He would win by any means, but he would win.

"What would happen is, say, East High School or another Salt Lake school's debate team would come to your high school and for four periods—social science, English, whatever—there would be a debate," said Cary Jones, a Salt Lake City lawyer who was a fellow debater in high school. "Kids would stand up in class with judges in the classroom, typically parents or whatever. And you literally spoke before every student in the school, maybe five times a year."

Along the way, Rove developed some tricks for victory.

One was the house of cards, which he used with some regularity. Rove closed the debate by pulling from his suit pocket a dozen playing cards and, as he recalled the arguments of the opposing team, he balanced the cards precariously on the table. Then, he paused.

After a beat, Rove seized on some errant fact, some soft point in the opponents' presentation, and in a dramatic flourish, pulled out a card to send the other team's whole argument tumbling to the table.

Fellow student Eric Kiesler said the moment was as engaging as an athletic event.

"When Karl was done, the crowd was fired up and cheering. The crowd reaction was comparable to having one of our sports teams win the state championship. It was amazing."

Once, Rove put on sunglasses and carried a cane, pretending to be blind as he built his case, fact by fact. He stumbled about the room, leading the student audience away from the flaws of his opponent's argument and to the logic of his own, out of the darkness and into the light. Finally, his audience persuaded, he pulled off his sunglasses and threw down the cane.

"Now you see!" he declared triumphantly.

"It was theater," according to classmate Mark Gustavson.

Senior year, the topic was compulsory military service. The draft. Few subjects had such power at that moment on high school and colleges campuses. The boys of Olympus High, like those everywhere, were nervously aware of the sharp divisions caused by

Vietnam and the how American involvement in that distant war was about to affect their lives.

"We were all so worried about being drafted," said classmate Rick Higgins.

The war was front-page news in the Salt Lake Tribune every day, on the network news every night. In January 1968, communist forces launched the Tet offensive on Hue and other major South Vietnam towns. By February, General William Westmoreland had requested 206,000 more troops. At home, there were draft card burnings and antiwar protests.

Curiously, Rove's view at the time was not so different, according to classmates. Rove had doubts about the war—which after all, was being prosecuted by a Democrat, Lyndon Johnson. In any case, he felt government had no right to require citizens to serve in the military.

He and classmate Mark Gustavson sat by the huge windows in the cafeteria discussing the issue.

"He was opposed to compulsory service. He felt we don't need the damn government telling us what to do. We can do it on our own."

According to Gustavson, Rove had reached his conclusion not from the left, but the right—as an expression of libertarianism. Supporting the war was equivalent to supporting big government and the intrusions of big government, especially the bloated, post-New Deal government of LBJ and Hubert Humphrey and the rest of the liberal Washington establishment. Whether guided more by the apprehension of being drafted or a commitment to individual liberty— Rove was no fan of the war, or at least the draft. Decades later, however, as the president's most critical advisor, Rove's policy direction and political moves contradicted these fundamental beliefs. He saw war in Iraq as essential and, as U.S. military forces were stretched thin by drawing down reserves and calling up the National Guard, he had to confront the potential need for a military draft.

He brought unbridled political passion to the topic of compulsory military service when he was a young man, though, winning debate after debate in classrooms of receptive draft-age high school students. He used what he called the "Mom, apple pie, and flag defense," meaning the position of the true American patriot. It was a fine piece of rhetorical jujitsu, friends remembered, which allowed Rove to reconcile opposition to the draft with conservative principle.

"I think there was a flag behind Karl. He brought in some cherry pie one day and handed out pieces of cherry pie to everyone. It was one of those one-upsmanships that would make the opponent think, 'where the hell do we go from here?'" said Gustavson.

There is a picture of Rove with the debate club in the 1969 high school yearbook, his senior year. He is seated in the first row and around him are his fellow debaters, mostly young men in spectacles and open-collar shirts. Rove is in a suit and tie. He is wearing an exuberant grin and is perched like a bundle of potential energy, as if he wants to burst out of the picture. Next to him, with her hand placed lightly on his knee as if to keep him from moving, is the faculty advisor, Diana Childs. She has the look of a teacher weary of trying to contain a hopelessly excitable terrier. Rove's mouth is open. Even here, at the moment the camera takes the picture, he is talking.

In the section highlighting student body officers, there is also a shot of Karl Rove, president of the student senate. It says: "Talking, reading, talking, writing speeches, talking, talking, talking—sometimes brilliant, sometimes verbose. Coming or going, constantly on the move. A doer instead of a watcher; vitally concerned, ever-debating, a mighty funny, never-stopped-to-ponder kind of guy."

Eldon Tolman's history class was made for students who liked to talk. Tolman wore a bow tie and glasses and he had a large, bony forehead and the imperious glare of a headmaster. He prodded students to talk in class, pushing and baiting them to express their views and then to defend them. He was a New Deal Democrat, an unreconstructed liberal. Tolman taught advanced placement history and government classes. He encouraged discussion, but Rove tested his limits. Once, he and a fellow student were so vociferous, refusing to shut up, that an exasperated Tolman ordered them both out of class.

Still, he saw instantly in Rove something he valued, a student passionate about the art of politics.

"Mr. Rove," Tolman announced one day, "it will be easy for you to get an A in this class, but to get an A you must join a campaign. I care not which."

It was an offer Rove could not refuse. He went down to Republican Party headquarters and signed up as a volunteer for the reelection campaign of Senator Wallace Bennett. He ran errands, erected lawn signs, knocked on doors, and distributed campaign literature. Around Halloween, he passed out pamphlets that said: "The Great Pumpkin says Vote for Wallace F. Bennett." It occurred to him how a message could be so simple, yet effective. He hung around the executive director's office a lot, interjecting himself into discussions about phone banks and political mailings. He became a regular habitué at GOP headquarters, a skinny little 17-year-old—"130 pounds, soaking wet," a friend said—with little experience and lots of ideas.

Randy Ludlow, another high school volunteer, said Rove wanted in on the big stuff from the beginning.

"Karl was down at campaign headquarters day in and day out. They would be strategizing and Karl would come up with different ideas and plans. They'd send him off to get coffee and donuts."

At school, Rove wore his Republicanism on his sleeve. One day at assembly, he introduced Governor Calvin Rampton, a moderate Democrat, with a jab at his politics.

The moment was startling.

Rove was trying to be funny, as if introducing a political peer. But he was a teenager and the governor was a guest and, according to some in the audience, it apparently occurred to everyone except Rove that he was no equal to a political figure who had been governor since 1965 and who was to become one of the most popular chief executives in Utah history, winning reelection twice. The photo of the event in the yearbook showed Rove accompanying an exasperated-looking Rampton, looking all the world like a man trying to escape his escort.

Whatever his charm to some people, Rove was irritating to others. "He annoyed a number of students," recalled Mike Gustavson.

Rove did not get the best grades in school. He was not among the top 3 percent, not a member of the National Honor Society. But he wielded a facile rhetoric, which he used like a weapon.

"Karl was a little guy but you didn't mess with him because Karl had a very sharp tongue," said classmate Chris Smart, now the editor of a weekly newspaper in Salt Lake City. "If you were going to give Karl some crap, you knew it was coming back at you. He was quick-witted and had a quick tongue."

The first time Rove saw a presidential race close up was that year, when Richard Nixon, George Wallace, and Hubert Humphrey all campaigned at the Mormon Tabernacle. Wallace's visit to the vividly white environs of Salt Lake City brought an unsettling racist appeal.

"Wallace was the first time I saw bigotry," Rove said. "Wallace was just ugly and vicious and mean. I will never forget the roar of the crowd when he said, 'If they lay down in front of my car, it'll be the last time.' The crowd just roared in hatred. And it astonished me."

The visit by the vice president was a particularly memorable moment. His entourage arrived at the Mormon Tabernacle late in the campaign, under a bright Western sun. It was hot, September 30, the final weeks of the 1968 presidential contest. And here came Hubert Humphrey—Happy Hubert—into the rarefied air of Republican Utah, into the prim heart of the Mormon Church. Rove was exuberant at the prospect of seeing a national political candidate in the flesh, even if it was the enemy. He was excited to see the apparatus of a national campaign, how a candidate entered the hall, the swarm of the press, the positioning of the Secret Service.

Tolman wanted his entire class to see the speech, so he commandeered a school bus to transport everybody. The class arrived early and was to take a spot near the back of the Tabernacle, squeezed in among a crowd of thousands. But first, the students milled about outside for a while as the school buses arrived and streams of staid and proper Mormons made their way into the building. This was perfect because Rove had decided before leaving that he would not just attend the speech; he would launch a protest outside.

"Karl and I immediately got into trouble with some Democrat supporters outside the Tabernacle," Gustavson said.

For one thing, Rove had printed up and distributed buttons, which he was wearing proudly on his suit coat. They said "Hubert Humphrey" with a line drawn through the name, and he pinned them on his lapel, turned upside down in the universal sign of distress.

Gustavson described reactions to Rove's approach as fairly predictable.

"I remember an older woman coming up, first accosting Karl and then me, blowing her stack at us for being disrespectful young people who were there to disrupt everything."

Rove was delighted. He stood in the bright sun in his suit and tie, a stone's throw from Temple Square, and shouted contempt for the policies of Lyndon Johnson and his henchman, Hubert Humphrey. Somebody yelled at Rove and he yelled back.

"Nixon's the one!" he shouted. "Nixon's the one!"

"There was a banner or two or a sign," Gustavson said. "We were loudly advocating against Lyndon Johnson's war, his revised New Deal politics and economics. The Democrats were down there in force and vociferous. It was quite a Hyde Park scene, very loud, very strident public debate outside Temple Square. It was great. We were giving them hell."

Rove said he cannot recall the protest; the man who can remember dates he thought about taking pictures off his office wall or the names of precinct chairmen in remote Idaho counties could not recall his first political demonstration.

Republican Wallace Bennett won election that fall to his fourth and final term as senator. Democrat Calvin Rampton buried his opponent for governor nearly two-to-one. And the

New Nixon—Rove's candidate—took Utah with 55 percent of the vote and carried a narrow national victory to Washington where, a few years later in the political wreckage of Watergate, Rove first met George W. Bush, the man who was to take him to the White House.

The thing that seemed so odd to some of his classmates was how wedded Rove was to the Republican Party, how he had attached himself so early to the hoary apparatus of the party.

"I always viewed the Republican Party as the party of my parents. And who wanted anything to do with that?" said classmate Cary Jones.

But there was something in the party that appealed to Rove, something solid and stable. The strong and muscular message—defense of home and hearth, discipline, order. The Democrats were the party of giveaways and lassitude. All around him was division. Salt Lake City was divided between those who were Mormon and those who were not. The nation was divided over Vietnam. His home was coming apart. His father was away much of the time and even when his parents were together, they argued. In a city where the prevalent influences were political and religious, his family was neither. He grew up in an apolitical household, without religious mooring.

Friend Mark Dangerfield told a reporter that it seemed to bother Rove that "he was raised in a completely nonreligious home."

His father, Louis, took a job in California with the mineral department of an oil company, and commuted. The plan, so far as Rove knew, was that the family would move to Los Angeles, but that never happened. In December 1969, his father came in, his parents fought, and Louis turned around and left for good. It was Christmas Eve. By the time he entered college, his parents were divorcing. Rove was 20 before he learned that Louis was actually his stepfather. He never knew his biological father until decades later and an attempt at reconciliation had failed. After the divorce, his mother moved to Reno and, some years later, she killed herself.

When Keith Roark came home from Vietnam, he picked up a copy of the student newspaper at the University of Utah and saw Karl Rove's name. Roark, the captain of the high school debate team Rove's sophomore year, had volunteered for the draft, joined the Army and gone to Vietnam. When he returned, he enrolled at the University of Utah. And it was there on campus in 1971 that he sat down with the campus newspaper one day and saw the name of Karl Rove, president of the University of Utah College Republicans.

"I was amazed that in the two years I had been gone, how many people who sort of had Republican leanings had become fervent anti-Nixon, anti-Republican. But not Karl Rove. Antiwar sentiment, even at the University of Utah, was rife. We're talking about the era of huge antiwar protests and hippies and marijuana and communes and alternative lifestyles. And Karl, as far as I know, never even winked in that direction. He set a course that he never wavered from, not even momentarily."

As a freshman at Utah, Rove got involved with something called the Hinckley Institute, which offered students an opportunity for internships both at the state capital and in Washington. The institute was an adjunct of the political science department on campus. It was created by Bob Hinckley, an old New Dealer who overcame a palpable resistance by the administration to the study of practical politics with a check for $250,000 for creation of an institute. His motto: Every student a politician.

When J. D. Williams first saw Rove his freshman year, he knew he had a live wire. Williams was the director of the Hinckley Institute, a venerated professor with a strong progressive streak—"My mortal gods are Thomas Jefferson, Franklin D. Roosevelt, and Martin Luther King."—who became the second academic liberal to take Rove under his wing. Since the founding of the institute in 1965, Williams had not seen a student so interested in the application of practical politics. Rove threw himself into his internship at the Statehouse and in Washington.

"I always felt a little guilty about the fact that he got so carried away with these political activities that he never graduated," said Williams, now professor emeritus.

Rove never got a college degree. He attended several colleges and eventually taught at the University of Texas, but the lure of practicing politics always outstripped his studies.

During the antiwar years, there was no tougher place to practice Republican politics than on a college campus. Rove had come to the attention of the hierarchy of the College Republicans, who dispatched him in 1970 to Illinois to organize campuses for Senator Ralph Smith, an old-line conservative who had been appointed to the job upon the death of the venerable Everett Dirksen. His opponent was Adlai Stevenson III.

"It was at the height of the Vietnam War. Ralph was an extremely conservative guy. It was, shall we say, an uphill climb," said Bob Kjellander, then president of the College Republican chapter at the University of Illinois.

Rove had all kinds of ideas, according to Kjellander. Dormitory canvasses. Precinct organizations on campus. Dorm chairmen. Floor chairmen. Rove traveled from school to school, from Champaign to Bloomington to Springfield. He formed a willing and ready alliance with the Young Americans for Freedom (YAF), the shock troops of the new right on college campuses. And they considered dirty tricks a part of the political process, an idea Karl Rove put into practice early in his career.

The Democratic candidate for state treasurer in 1970 was Alan Dixon, a likable Illinois politician who was climbing the political ladder that was eventually to lead him to a seat in the U.S. Senate. The Dixon for Treasurer Campaign planned to formally open its Chicago headquarters with a flourish, inviting party officials, the press, and supporters.

Rove had an idea: Disrupt the opening.

He assumed a false name and posed as a supporter to get into campaign headquarters, where he stole some Dixon campaign stationary.

Rove used the stationary to fake an invitation to the opening, giving the correct time and place, but adding, "Free beer, free food, girls, and a good time for nothing." He made 1,000 copies and distributed them at a hippie commune, a rock concert, soup kitchens, and among the drunks on Chicago's bowery. And it worked. On the day of the opening, hundreds of the city's dissolute showed up. Vans arrived with freeloaders attracted by the promise of liquor and food.

"It was funny," Kjellander remembered. "He had all these winos showing up at a fancy party with an open bar."

Dixon had a decidedly different view.

"It was a little upsetting."

Still, Dixon won and he has subsequently dismissed the episode as a minor inconvenience. Although Kjellander recalled that Rove was eventually directed by George Herbert Walker Bush to apologize, Dixon has no memory of receiving an apology.

"I don't recall ever being in Karl Rove's presence. Maybe I was, but I don't recall it," said Dixon, who left the Senate in 1993 and is now an attorney in St. Louis.

He added crisply, "I gather that Karl Rove has become a rather important political operative."

Rove rose swiftly in the hierarchy of College Republicans during the early 1970s, eventually becoming executive director, a staff job with an office at the Republican National Committee and an annual salary of $9,200. He organized 15 regional conferences to instruct young Republicans on the gears and levers of practical politics. Rove and colleague Bernie Robinson traveled the country, to San Diego, West Virginia, Wisconsin, American University in Washington. Mostly the sessions were about organization and message, but Rove could not resist instructing his young audiences on dirty tricks—pranks, he called them.

At a seminar in Lexington, Kentucky, in August 1972, Rove and Robinson recounted the Dixon episode with considerable delight. They talked about campaign espionage, about digging through an opponent's garbage for intelligence—then using it against them.

Robinson recounted how that technique had worked well for him in the 1968 governor's race in Illinois when he "struck gold" in a search of an opponent's stolen garbage. He found evidence that a supporter had given checks to both sides in the race, but more to the Democrat, Sam Shapiro.

"So one of our finance guys calls the guy up the next day and told him there was a vicious rumor going around," Robinson said, according to a tape recording of the seminar. "The guy got all embarrassed and flew to Chicago that day with a check for $2,000 to make up the difference," he said.

This was the summer of the Watergate break-in, with the first revelations of a scandal that unraveled the Nixon presidency. The Watergate burglars broke into the Democratic National Committee offices on June 17 and the whole business of political dirty tricks was rapidly becoming a very sensitive subject. Both Rove and Robinson recognized that. They even specifically mentioned the Watergate break-in at the seminars, not as a reason to avoid campaign espionage, but as a caution to keep it secret.

"Again in those things, if it's used surreptitiously in a campaign, it's better if you don't get caught. You know, those people who were caught by Larry O'Brien's troops in Washington are a serious verification of the fact that you don't get caught," Robinson added.

That was the message: Don't get caught. And there was this swaggering attitude about it, the whole exuberant Young Republican thing: We're young and indestructible and there's nothing so much fun as full-contact politics with a faint menace of danger.

Nobody expressed this better than Lee Atwater, who was about to emerge on the national scene as the bad boy of testosterone politics. Rove had never seen anybody quite like Lee, with his slow-cured manner and take-no-prisoners attitude. Atwater read the New York Times and the National Enquirer. He quoted Sun-Tzu. ("If your opponent is of choleric temper, seek to irritate him.") He was everything Rove wanted to be: the perfect political warrior.

In 1973, when Rove was recruited to run for chairman of the College Republican National Committee, a group of supporters paired him with Atwater, who at the time was president of the College Republicans in South Carolina. Rove was to be the candidate and Atwater his Southern campaign chairman. In March, Rove took the train from Washington to Columbia, South Carolina, a $25 overnight ticket, where he was met by Atwater and another young hardball Republican, John Carbaugh, later to become advisor to Jesse Helms. With a Gulf credit card, Rove and Atwater rented a mustard-brown Ford Pinto and proceeded to spend the next week campaigning together across the South, visiting state college Republican chairmen, and asking for support.

The deal went like this: Rove was to be chairman and Atwater would take his old job, executive director of the College Republican National Committee. Both of them would be in Washington with an office and a phone and the run of the Republican National Committee (RNC). It was impossible not to like Atwater. He was fun loving and amiable and he was forever scheming about one thing or the other. The two of them had barely taken their new jobs in Washington, Rove said, before Atwater was hustling Republican National Committee Chairman George H. W. Bush for use of his boat.

Rove was awestruck by Atwater's self-confidence.

"I introduced Lee to George Bush. Lee wanted to meet George Bush because he was chairman but also because he'd heard that the chairman had a boat that he kept on the Potomac. Lee had a big date lined up for the weekend and he thought it would be very impressive if he could take this little Strom Thurmond intern named Sally out on the Potomac on George Bush's boat.

"So—classic Atwater—five minutes after he has met the chairman of the Republican National Committee, he was bumming the use of his boat. And the audacious guy he was, he got it."

But to get to Washington, they had to win, and to win, they had to out-politick the other guys. The two of them—Rove and

Atwater—crisscrossed the South in the spring of 1973 lining up support in advance of the summer convention where the new chairman of the College Republicans was to be chosen. Atwater knew all the fronts and fissures of campus politics in the region, who was important and who was not. By the time they rolled into Lake of the Ozarks in June for the convention, Atwater and Rove had a battle plan. And in the end, according to his opponent, Rove had to steal the election to win.

The hotel in Lake of the Ozarks was swarming with young Republicans. There were sessions on practical politics in the little meeting rooms and politicking in the hallways, particularly for the election of the new national chairman. Atwater and Rove cruised the rooms and the bar, looking to lock up votes. There were three candidates: Rove; Robert Edgeworth, a Goldwater devotee who had headed up Students for Nixon at the University of Michigan; and Terry Dolan, the future founder of the National Conservative Political Action Committee. Dolan, whose acerbic personality made it difficult to round up support, realized that he didn't have the votes to win and threw in with Edgeworth.

It was a two-man race for a majority of the votes. But which votes? Rove and Atwater's plan, supported by a faction within the College Republicans sometimes called the Chicago Boys, took as a point of pride its influence on the gears and levers of the organization. Atwater and the Chicago Boys decided the best way to win an election was to make sure the votes that counted were their votes. There was suddenly a flurry of challenges at the credentials committee, which went into the night.

"The credentials committee savagely went through and threw out, often on the flimsiest of reasons, most of my supporters," said Edgeworth, who steered his own campaign with a bullhorn and a stack of proxies, which challenged Rove and Atwater.

Tempers flared and there were near-fistfights. Edgeworth supporters shouted at Rove's people, who shouted back. The committee was stymied. The next day, with everybody gathered in a large hall, Rove's name was entered into nomination, and as the roll was called, region-by-region, one voice shouted "Aye" and another voice yelled "No." Then, against a chorus of boos and cheers, Edgeworth was also nominated, just as Rove had been, and the same thing happened. Each side declared victory.

"I gave a nice acceptance speech, thanking everybody for electing me. Then I sat down," said Edgeworth. "Karl got up, gave a nice acceptance speech for everybody who had elected him. Then we both went to Washington, DC."

The issue was to be decided by RNC Chairman George Bush. Both sides made their cases, but Rove seemed to have an advantage, having already met Bush while working as executive director of the College Republicans. Before Bush had announced his decision, Dolan went to the media with some particularly damning material about Rove—tapes and transcripts of the "dirty tricks" seminars.

"I forbade him to but he did it anyway," Edgeworth said.

The *Washington Post* published the story under the headline *"GOP Probes Official as Teacher of Tricks."* This was exactly the kind of publicity the Republican party did not need. The storm clouds were building over Watergate. The Senate was investigating. Nixon had announced in April the departure of John Dean, John Haldeman, and John Ehrlichman. And now George Bush, who as chairman of the party had pledged to keep the GOP free of Watergate taint, was having to deal with a published report in the Washington Post—adjacent to the day's Watergate investigation story, for god's sake—about tape recordings and "dirty tricks" workshops by a GOP college operative.

In fact, the evidence had been given first to the RNC and quietly reviewed by a committee and dismissed. Only afterward did the tapes and affidavits find their way into the media. Now in the bright light of a newspaper report, Bush promised to reopen the inquiry. Three weeks later, September 6, he sent a letter to both candidates declaring Rove the winner.

Edgeworth wrote back asking on what basis Bush had made the decision—and got a blistering reply.

"He sent me back an absolutely furious letter in which he wrote me out of the party. He said he certainly would not answer such impertinent inquiries from someone who was disloyal to the party and leaked hostile information to the press, which I had never done."

The response was odd, Edgeworth thought. Bush was angry not because a Republican had conducted seminars on campaign espionage, but because someone had gone to the press with the story. Obviously, the priority was containing the scandal, not getting to the bottom of it. This was all about loyalty and the club; no true Republican would violate the party code by going to the media. That was the message that Edgeworth heard.

A few months later, Bush hired Rove as his special assistant at the RNC.

How perfect was this? Assistant to the chairman of the Republican National Committee. Back at Olympus High, Rove had talked with his friend Randy Ludlow about how he was going to Washington, and now he was here, in the big time. Every morning when Chairman Bush arrived at the basement parking garage and stepped into the elevator, rising to the fourth floor, Rove was there eagerly ready for the day. As a member of the personal staff, Rove had all the authority of an assistant to the RNC chairman—which is to say, not much authority at all. Mostly he was a gopher. But the place was the center of the Republican universe, a place to make associations and stay current on the party's latest line.

His most important association, although he didn't know it then, was the boss' son, George W. Bush.

Defining moments of lives are often nothing more than chance encounters. But Karl Rove was leaving nothing to providence, in this case. When it came to George W. Bush, Rove ended up taking chance out of the equation. And in the process, he changed—not just their lives—but also American history.

8

Gone to Texas

Let your secret sympathies and your compassion be always with the under dog in the fight—this is magnanimity; but bet on the other one—this is business.

—Mark Twain

Envy and maybe even a bit of idolatry led to the relationship that spawned the presidency of George W. Bush. Nothing more complex happened than a geek meeting a cool guy. And the geek, who knew he could never be like the cool guy, decided to hang out with him and help him be even cooler. Maybe that was a way for him to find self-worth or a kind of affirmation that, in a small way, he too was cool. No matter what that friendship was to give Karl Rove, it gave America a presidency and a sociopolitical transformation that will confound historians and political scientists for decades.

And it all began very innocently.

Karl Rove's new friend was a lot of things he was not. George W. had graduated from Yale and served a stint as a pilot with the Texas Air National Guard, and now he was a graduate student at Harvard Business School, and from time to time he came to Washington to see his parents and to check out the nightlife with friends. The younger Bush had a kind of easy, almost indifferent, quality. He wore a leather flight jacket, had brown hair and blue eyes and a bronze complexion. He blew gum bubbles while he waited to see his dad. Rove remembered his first impression.

"He was . . . cool."

Rove's task in those days was simple enough.

"I was supposed to give him the car keys whenever he came to town."

The Republican National Committee was a perfect place to make political associations and soak in the influences of Washington, the greatest political city in the world. His strongest influence was Atwater. Both Rove and Lee Atwater had illusions of political stardom, but it was Atwater who first made his name in Washington. He reminded Rove of one of those Southern stock cars exploding with noise and energy and going 150 miles an hour. Lee carried himself with colossal self-confidence, no matter where—greeting a group of blue-chip political donors or drinking with friends at a Georgetown bar.

Rove knew he could never match that.

"We're not alike. He had an incredible gut instinct for how ordinary people would react. I guess I'm more cerebral, he's more gut," Rove said.

The thing that most impressed Rove was the sharp intelligence Atwater brought to the game of politics. That, and what Rove called his friend's "understanding of the thrust and parry of the negative." Atwater looked at politics like war. He liked to say he read "The Prince" by Machiavelli every year.

"Lee had a great knack to visualize," said Richard McBride, a Republican consultant and friend to both Atwater and Rove.

"His whole thing was wedges and magnets. What pulls people apart and what attracts people? You drive wedges and you find magnets. You find ways to bring people to you and ways to divide people who are against you."

Atwater rose like a rocket in political Washington, from deputy assistant for political affairs in the Reagan White House to architect of George Bush's 1988 presidential victory to chairman of the Republican National Committee. All by the age of 40. Rove maintained close ties with Atwater even after circumstances led him to Texas, where he watched his old friend's ascension with no small measure of envy.

At dinner one night in Austin, Atwater told Rove, "Karl, you should be up in DC as a strategist like me."

But by then, he'd already set his roots deeply in Texas. While working for Bush in Washington, Rove had met the daughter of a Houston barge broker, Valerie Wainright, and in July 1976 they were married. Valerie's grandmother had been a matriarch of Houston society in the 1940s and 1950s and her family had founded the Houston social register. Valerie was groomed as part of the Republican WASP establishment in Houston, and Rove was a young Republican on the rise, working at that time as finance director for the Virginia state party and a deputy in President Ford's election campaign.

The Virginia Republican party was in debt; the most money it had ever raised was $110,000 in 1972. Rove, who had no particular expertise in raising money, was dispatched to Richmond, where he found himself walking around the Fidelity Building wondering how he—a 26-year-old living from paycheck to paycheck—was going to raise money for a party that didn't even have a fund-raiser on its schedule.

He did have one thing: a magnetic tape with the names of 30,000 past contributors.

And with that, Rove was in the direct-mail business. Within a year, he had raised more than $400,000 and put the party in the black. But his job, like always, consumed much of his time and energy and Valerie was unhappy with Richmond and wanted to return to Houston. So in November, after Jimmy Carter and the Democrats reclaimed the White House, Karl and Valerie moved to Texas, but the threads of their marriage were rapidly unraveling.

As it turned out, Texas was the perfect proving ground for Rove to develop politically. He stayed close to the Bush family, helping the elder Bush with his new political action committee, the Fund for Limited Government, and assisting the son in his 1978 race for Congress.

Rove set up shop at 1801 Main Street in Houston, and in the beginning, he was the staff—arranging schedules, producing a political newsletter, and cultivating the lists of Republican financial donors who were the mother's milk of any presidential bid. Mostly, the job was traveling. James A. Baker III lent his name as chairman of the committee, but the committee at first was really only three people—Rove, a pilot, and Bush—in pursuit of support from the golden money guys in the glass towers and energy company offices and corn-belt congressional districts in states that elect Republican presidents. Later, Margaret Tutweiler and Jennifer Fitzgerald joined the staff.

Out on the level landscape of West Texas, a kind of referendum on Reagan-Bush was already underway. While the father was pursing the presidency under the colors of his political action committee, the son had decided to run for the nineteenth congressional seat. The district's venerable old Democratic congressman, who had held seat for nearly a half century, had announced his retirement and George W. jumped into the race. At 32 and a newcomer to the oil business in Midland, the younger Bush presented a clear target for political rivals out on this parched stretch of oil and cotton country.

"He's a personable young man from back East," said his Republican primary opponent, Jim Reese.

The operable words hung in the air like an obscenity. Back East. As in Yankee blue-blood New York City effete.

Reese was a stockbroker and former mayor of Odessa. He was also a vigorous Reagan Republican, and Reagan showed his appreciation by sending along a letter of endorsement, which Reese mass-mailed to every Republican in the district and half the Democrats, too. Reagan's political action committee, Citizens for the Republic, sent money and Reagan surrogates dropped into the district to speak on Reese's behalf. At the Petroleum Club in Midland, everybody was for young George. But the district was more than Midland. It stretched for 17 counties across a largely rural constituency from Friona to Farwell where farmers and roughnecks and small-town shopkeepers were no stranger to hard work and to the red-dust storms that could soil a line of clothes in an instant and turn the windows black.

The elder Bush directed Rove to get involved. Although paid from the father's political action committee, Rove became an informal advisor in the son's congressional bid, offering strategic advice and helping organize fund-raisers hosted by the father in Washington, Dallas, Houston, and Midland. Rove had become a master technician of Republican money, and money flowed into George W.'s campaign treasury.

On the stump, Reese pressed the case that George W. was a carpetbagger, born in New Haven, Connecticut, and educated in the pointy-headed environs of Harvard and Yale.

He even made Rove an issue.

"I am very disappointed that he has Rockefeller-type Republicans such as Karl Rove to help him run his campaign," he said in a letter to voters.

But George W. won the primary and the right to face Democrat Kent Hance, a graduate of Texas Tech who played the good-old-boy card with all the smoothness of a small-town cattle broker. Hance graduated from Dimmitt High School; Bush graduated from a private prep school in Massachusetts.

Case closed.

Bush lost the general election by more than 6,000 votes.

Reese offered a prescient coda, "He has a bright future in politics somewhere, but it's not out here."

Two things were to distinguish all future Bush political campaigns: Karl Rove would be totally in charge and Bush would never lose again.

Whatever assistance Rove gave George W. in 1978, his attention was primarily on the father and his pre-presidential effort. The elder Bush's itinerary in 1978 included 135 political events in 41 states, a flurry of plane flights and van rides with Bush out front and Rove scurrying at his side in a gray suit, carrying an over-stuffed valise.

In 1979, Valerie filed for divorce. The climatic moment, Rove recalled, was the counseling session at the Episcopal Church where a trendy young priest in jeans and boots opened the session in a gentle, conciliatory tone.

"Okay, here are the ground rules," he said.

Rove fidgeted in his chair; Valerie sat nervously smoking a cigarette. Before the priest could finish the ground rules, Valerie was up.

"Wait a minute," she said. "I don't know why I'm here. I don't love you. I've never loved you. And I'm leaving."

With that, she walked out. It was like a thunderclap, then a long silence. She had never loved him. His marriage had failed; he had failed. The priest slowly picked up his notebook and looked over at Rove, who sat shaking, angry, and humiliated.

"Well," the priest said, closing his notebook, "that about says it all."

In the summer in Austin, the sun blazes with a white-hot intensity, making the grass brittle and creating heat waves that rise like liquid off the concrete. Along Shoal Creek, on a thin stretch of land, shirtless college students in sandals play Frisbee golf even in the hard heat of September. You can see them playing from the windows of Karl Rove's direct-mail office, where he set up shop a couple of years after the divorce and where, in September 1985, he sat down and wrote an important memo.

George W. Bush's road to the White House could not have happened without the resurgence of the Republican Party in Texas, which began with a memo by Karl Rove. Texas was rock-solid Democrat. For 100 years, from the end of Reconstruction to the passage of the 1965 Voting Rights Act, Democrats owned the South and Texas was part of the South. They had a phrase for it in East Texas, "yellow dog Democrat," meaning you would vote for a yellow dog before you'd ever vote for a Republican in a political race.

In Texas, there had been the occasional Republican success—John Tower replacing Lyndon Johnson in the U.S. Senate in 1961 and Dallas oilman Bill Clements in 1978 becoming the first Republican in a century to be governor. But in the 1982 elections, every statewide Republican candidate lost, including Clements, and it appeared the Democratic Party had reasserted its long hold on Texas politics.

No way, Karl Rove thought. Something was happening in the shifting demographics of Texas, and he saw it. The Sun Belt had become a magnet for a new economy and a new workforce attracted by factories, high-tech, and corporate relocations. Nationally, Ronald Reagan was the instrument of the political realignment. He was virile and optimistic, the poster boy for "Morning in America," and he was making the Republican party respectable to millions of Southern whites and a wave of upwardly mobile new arrivals.

So Rove sat down in his chair on a white-hot September day, under a portrait of his political patron saint Teddy Roosevelt, and he composed a memo.

"It's important to start with a clear understanding of where we are today," he wrote.

The memo outlined a strategy for Bill Clements, who had won and lost the governorship, to win it again. Clements had proved an unpopular governor, strong-willed and difficult. He had made a fortune in the rigorous business of drilling for oil and carried into his first term a tendency to treat other elected officials as paid employees, not political peers. In 1982, he was turned out by Attorney General Mark White in a Democratic tide that also swept Ann Richards into her first statewide office as state treasurer.

Rove outlined Clements' strengths, largely that people knew who he was, and his weaknesses, which were considerable. He said people saw Clements as mean and insensitive and the media would write that the former governor wanted a rematch against White for revenge. It was all dead-on accurate. The key, Rove wrote, was to turn everything upside down by softening Clements' image and defusing the idea that he was a bad loser.

Then he wrote:

The whole art of war consists in a well-reasoned and extremely circumspect defensive, followed by rapid and audacious attack.

—Napoleon.

He went back and highlighted Napoleon's words. Rapid. Audacious. Attack. But first, he said, the best defense was for Clements to
highlight his record and rehabilitate himself by acknowledging in a
humorous, self-effacing way, that he had learned from his mistakes.
The new suburbanites would vote for Clements, Rove knew, but
only if he seemed sensitive to their interests.

"The purpose of saying you gave teachers a record pay increase
is to reassure suburban voters with kids, not to win the votes of
teachers," the memo said.

Rove understood the potential of the state's changing demographics and he understood Clements. When Rove's marriage was
failing in 1979, he moved to Austin and took a job in the new governor's political office, which he pursued with a voracious energy. His
job was to manage the campaign-contributor lists and edit new fund-
raising appeals for Clements. In short order, he created the gold standard of political lists, a road map of Republican mega-money guys.

Rove set up his own direct-mail business in 1981. A year later,
his first client was the Bill Clements for Governor reelection campaign. Clements lost but the mailing lists were acquired by Rove and
proved invaluable. Nobody had better files than Rove on big dog
Republican donors and he used them both to lure political clients
and to expand his business into fund-raising for museums like the
trendy Phillips Collection in Washington. The museum business
provided income independent of the fortunes of the Republican
Party, which were not particularly good at the moment in Texas.

"Until Karl came along, there was no real Republican consultant
of his stature in Texas," said George Christian, former White House
press secretary to Lyndon Johnson. "There wasn't anybody with an
overall concept. He could pretty much do it all."

The Democrats didn't know it, but Rove had designs on the entire statewide ticket. In little more than a decade, every Democrat in elective statewide office was gone, replaced by Republicans—virtually every one a Rove client.

"It was a cartel," said one Republican colleague.

Rove directed Clements' return to office with characteristic attention to detail: a month-by-month blueprint of how to paint incumbent Mark White as an incompetent, self-serving politico susceptible to defeat on Election Day.

"Anti-White messages are more important than positive Clements messages," Rove wrote in a strategy memo.

"Attack. Attack. Attack."

By happenstance or design, it all worked. The campaign's own polling numbers showed that Rove's strategy had given Clements a slender lead, but White was closing—until the bugging episode, which erupted with a flourish of publicity and fatally stalled White's rise.

The day of Clements' inaugural, the sky was thick with gray clouds and a biting wind. Rove threaded his way through the crowd, a happy man. Limos were double-parked in the street behind the Governor's Mansion, and on the portico, chrome coat racks stretched for yards festooned with mink, fox, and ermine. These were his guys, the golden mega-dollars guys from his computer lists, made manifest in the flesh. Rove had the contributors and now he began accumulating candidates: a young ex-legislator named Kay Bailey Hutchison for state treasurer, a Democrat-turned-Republican named Rick Perry for agriculture commissioner.

When Clements appointed a 39-year-old district judge from Houston named Tom Phillips to an opening as chief justice of the Texas Supreme Court, Rove instantly assumed him as a client.

"That sort of led people to feeling they could win something," said Harry Whittington, an Austin lawyer and long-time Republican.

"They went after the Supreme Court. I don't think anybody thought of that being such a political job, but Karl was the man who showed that it could be done."

Through appointment and election, Republicans gradually took over the high court. Like a ritual, the Republican hierarchy cleared all potential candidates through Rove, who then became their paid political consultant and steered money into their campaign accounts. For candidates who were largely unknown, Rove's imprimatur meant all the difference. It was perfect. Business got the judges it wanted, the Republican Party was winning elections and Rove got paid.

"Once the Republican leadership in Texas knew that Karl Rove was aboard, it put the mantle of endorsement on it," said Ralph Wayne, the amiable, silver-haired leader of an influential business group involved in vetting potential candidates.

When a Houston judge named Priscilla Owen called one day, asking for an appointment, Wayne asked what was on her mind.

"I'm thinking about running for Supreme Court," she said.

"Have you to talked to Karl Rove?" Wayne asked.

"No," said Owen, taking the hint. "But I plan to."

It turned out to be Priscilla Owen's smartest career move. She would later end up with an appointment to the federal bench when George W. Bush became president. Karl Rove recommended her.

There was one person Rove did not have under contract, somebody he'd begun to think would make a great candidate for governor: George W. Bush. Over the years, he and George W. had stayed in contact. Rove began talking up George W. Bush as a possible candidate for governor. During the elder Bush's inauguration, Rove made sure that certain folks knew there was another Bush on the political horizon. At a reception in Washington, a Republican congressman introduced Bush as the "next governor of Texas."

Bush took the lectern and joked, "I don't know what makes people in Texas think I'm considering it, just because we changed the names of our twins to Dallas and Fort Worth."

Bush was interested, buoyed by the picture that Rove painted of the state's political landscape, the favorable demographic shifts and weak Republican field for 1990.

Newspapers increasingly floated Bush's name as a potential candidate. He became the subject of running speculation among political operatives at the Texas Chili Parlor and the Austin Club.

Eventually, Rove's trial balloon went flat.

The White House sent word that it didn't want George W. to run. The fear was that the governor's race would become a referendum on the Bush presidency.

Instead, Republicans in 1990 chose a political novice named Clayton Williams, a jug-eared millionaire rancher from Midland with a penchant for saying the wrong thing at the wrong time. He opened the race with a politically incorrect joke about rape and ended it with an admission that he hadn't paid income taxes the previous year. Democrat Ann Richards, her political star rising fast, beat him easily in November, becoming only the second woman ever elected governor of Texas. But it was no Democrat sweep. Rove's candidates for treasurer and agriculture commissioner, Kay Bailey Hutchison and Rick Perry, both won.

The Perry race was particularly noteworthy. The dark-haired, handsome son of a West Texas rancher, Perry had grown up a Democrat and served in the Legislature, but Rove convinced him to switch political parties and run for higher office.

"He got Lee Atwater to send me a note. You know, 'Come over, the water's fine,'" said Perry, now governor of Texas.

Rove decided Perry should run for agriculture commissioner. His opponent was the incumbent, Jim Hightower, a formidable figure in populist circles.

"I think Karl saw it as great sport that he was trying to beat Hightower with this young, three-term House member."

The contest had all the signature marks of an Atwater campaign, including the wedge issues of patriotism and race. Hightower said he saw no need to outlaw flag burning in the Constitution, so Rove recruited

Senator Orrin Hatch of Utah, sponsor of a constitutional amendment against flag burning, to visit Texas on Perry's behalf. Hightower had supported the Rev. Jesse Jackson for president, so Rove flooded East Texas with mass mailings and a television commercial featuring Hightower and Jackson, their fists aloft in an image that seemed designed to coax a recollection of the Olympic black-power salute.

But the thing that truly caused Democrats to take note was the federal investigation. The last time the FBI got involved in a state political race was 1986, the bugging of the Clements' campaign office . . . Rove's office.

In both cases, Rove's clients were the beneficiaries.

A few weeks after word first appeared in the newspapers that a federal grand jury was investigating the agriculture department, Rove breezed into Perry headquarters and plopped down in a chair next to campaign manager Ken Luce. He outlined his plan for beating Hightower in typical Rove fashion—an avalanche of words, statistics, constituencies, demographic groups. A careful time line, month-by-month, issue-by-issue. Deploy the Farm Bureau. Peel off some voters here in East Texas, some votes there in West Texas. Flag burning. Jesse Jackson. Attack. Attack. Attack.

In a business where the politics of the day is paramount, Luce recalled that Rove was playing a very long game, planning not months, but years ahead. And as they sat there talking, Luce thought it odd that the candidate who most occupied Rove's thinking was not even a candidate at all, but George W. Bush, the new managing general partner of the Texas Rangers baseball team. Even then, in the spring of 1990, Rove had plans for George W. beyond the Governor's Mansion.

Luce remembered exactly what Rove said.

"If George wants to, George can be governor. George can be president."

"This is how it would work: If George were governor, he would have the state of Texas, a base. You have the electoral votes. You have the money. That's how you can launch a presidential bid."

And that's exactly what Rove and Bush ended up doing.

9

Refining the Crude

Education is hanging around until you've caught on.
—Robert Frost

A decade and a half before he became suspected of leaking an undercover CIA agent's name to reporters, Karl Rove was sharpening his skills of dissembling, leaking, and deceiving. In Texas, he parsed words to avoid answering questions. He was much better at it than President Clinton, a man Rove criticized years later for asking for a definition of "is." For Rove, all of life is political and there is only one purpose: to win the latest contest. And even when victory is not possible, he wants to leave his opponent bloodied by the conflict.

But there have only been a few times when Rove acknowledged he could be beaten. And they have helped to inform his philosophy as a political consultant.

A covey of Senate sergeants arranged the walnut tables carefully in the center of the chamber, making a long rectangle, like a scaffold. The room had the brittle energy of a hanging. Karl Rove stood in the back of the chamber between paintings of the fall of the

Alamo and the bloody victory at San Jacinto, looking across the floor sloping in the direction of the lieutenant governor's platform. In the high leather chairs where the state senators usually sat, there were lobbyists, reporters, and some members of the newly installed Ann Richards administration, drawn by the promise of a spectacle.

When the Texas Senate is not in session, its chamber is used for committee meetings, and on this day in March 1991 the Senate Nominations Committee met to consider the appointment of Karl Rove to the East Texas State University board of regents. Rove had been appointed by Governor Bill Clements before leaving office, but needed confirmation by the Democrat-controlled Senate. Traditionally, the committee approved the nominees of governors, even governors of the other party. But Rove had found his way onto the radar screen of Texas Democrats, who had questions. There was the bugging episode and the investigation of Hightower and the other election-year inquiries into Democrats that had the faint, acrid smell of political dirty tricks. At least, it looked that way to Democrats, so the chance to get Rove to sit down, under oath, was an opportunity to be taken.

"Mr. Rove," said Senator Bob Glasgow, "I have a few questions for you."

Glasgow was from Stephenville, dairy country. He had the thin look of a Calvinist, with a razor-straight jaw line and the glint of spectacles perched on the bridge of his nose. Glasgow was a lawyer, skilled in the art of questioning witnesses, so he led the assault on Rove.

"Mr. Rove, would you now tell us publicly who bugged your office that you blamed upon Mark White publicly and in the press statewide?"

"First of all," said Rove, "I did not blame it on Mark White. If you'll recall, I specifically said at the time that we disclosed the bugging that we did not know who did it, but we knew who might benefit from it. And no, I do not know."

Glasgow asked about FBI agent Greg Rampton, Rove parsed his answer by wanting the senator to provide a definition for the word "know," and they began loudly talking over each other until the chairman picked up his gavel and pounded on the table for order.

"In campaigns that you've been involved in," Glasgow pressed on, "do you know why agent Rampton conducted a criminal investigation of Garry Mauro at a time you were involved in the campaign, pulled the finance records of Bob Bullock at the time you were involved in that campaign, pulled the campaign records of Jim Hightower at the time you were involved in that campaign?"

Rove professed his innocence, said he didn't know much about the first two campaigns, barely knew Rampton. As for the FBI investigation of Hightower, he said it was prompted by newspaper stories, not by him. But it was all really beside the point. This Senate was going to reject his appointment. And the memory of it stayed with him. Years later, long after his political success had taken him from Texas into the White House, Rove still remembered how his enemies had come after him.

"I was going to make them do it," Rove said in Austin one day after visiting the president at his ranch in Crawford. "It was unfair and it was political and they wanted a pound of flesh. But I didn't want to give up and step aside. Let them do it for their reasons and put it out on the record."

In his study at home, Rove had built a wall of bookshelves with a ladder to accommodate a prodigious library. When Max Sherman, dean of the Lyndon B. Johnson (LBJ) School of Public Affairs in Austin asked Rove to teach a graduate class in American politics and political campaigns, he jumped at the chance. Rove was forever compensating for his lack of a formal degree, and teaching college students offered a kind of compensation. If others had graduate degrees and professional experience in education or criminal justice, Rove devoured books on his off-time with a manic passion that allowed him to debate on equal terms with the experts, first in Austin and later at the White House. There simply was no time to get a degree, much less earn a string of graduate degrees that were the solid-gold credentials of public policy. But he could learn on his own terms and he could teach.

So he snapped at the offer to teach at the LBJ School. And after Paul Begala was called back to Washington to help the beleaguered Clinton White House, Rove took his place teaching an undergraduate class on politics and press at the University of Texas. His teaching partner, *Austin American-Statesman* political columnist Dave McNeely, remembered Rove arriving from campaign flights and sitting down with a pile of memos, polling results, phone callback messages. Head down, writing, Rove seemed absorbed in his paperwork as students expounded on the historic lessons of the 1800 presidential race or McKinley's use of the mail in 1898.

"That's 1896." Rove's head was suddenly up; he'd been following every word. "There were 14 pieces of mail and publications for every voter who voted in the 1896 election—a Croatian-American list, the first mass-produced political publication in Yiddish. It was a pretty amazing campaign underneath the surface. . . ."

And Rove was off and running, connecting the threads of past scholarship with the details of this week's campaign, drowning the class in statistical data, painting the big picture. When asked in a lawsuit how it was that he could teach college without a degree, Rove said, "I'm very good at what I do." Without a doubt, he did value education and his appointment to the board of regents of a state university really meant something—and his rejection was an injury he likely would not forget.

George W. Bush went to all the best schools, Phillips Academy, Yale, Harvard Business School. His style—the Bush style—was not to master a broad range of subjects, but instead to confront issues as needed. If he needed to know something, he would learn it. Friends knew that he was smart, but no intellectual. He was, in fact, rigorously anti-intellectual, deeply suspicious of gratuitous intellectualism, which opponents sometimes misread as a lack of intelligence.

"He'd always wait until the last minute to write his paper," said college roommate Clay Johnson. "But he held his own academically both at Andover and Yale."

His college transcripts from Yale—published in the *New Yorker* during the presidential campaign—revealed that he never earned an A as an undergraduate, but never flunked a course, either. His grades most often reflected a "gentleman's C." He scored a 73 in Introduction to the American Political System, a 71 in Introduction to International Relations. In Spanish, which was to serve him well in his bid to touch every willing voter, he averaged 77.

"I wasn't exactly an Ivy League scholar," Bush told a reporter for Texas Monthly. "What I was good at was getting to know people."

Few jobs offered a better avenue for getting to know people—and getting people to know you—than managing general partner of the Texas Rangers baseball team. After his father won the White House in 1988, Bush moved his family back to Dallas, where a friend tipped him the team was for sale. Using family influence and affiliations, Bush helped organize the purchase of the Rangers, sold his Harken Energy stock to buy a piece of the deal, and emerged the team's most visible figure. He had a seat in the stands with the fans where he sat with his boots up on the railing, greeting kids, and signing autographs. But from his eleventh floor office, Bush saw something that disturbed him.

Just below, among the cluster of storefronts and office buildings, Ross Perot had opened his headquarters to run for president. Looking down, Bush saw a growing hive of activity. Cars filled the parking lot—new Cadillacs, Porsches, Mercedes-Benzes.

"These were our guys," Bush said, alarmed.

He repeatedly called Washington to warn that something was happening, that the Perot challenge to his father's reelection was real. But he said the campaign team didn't take Perot's third-party challenge seriously, not until it was too late.

"The irony is that his father's defeat in 1992 opens the door for 43 [younger Bush]," said Rove, as if it were an equation.

Roland Betts, a friend from Yale and partner in the Rangers deal, told a Houston Chronicle reporter that Bush made it clear one day the time just wasn't right.

"You know," Betts recalls Bush saying, "I could run for governor and all this but I'm basically a media creation. I've never really done anything. I've worked for my dad. I worked in the oil industry. But that's not the kind of profile you have to have to get elected to public office."

The Rangers job changed all that. He had successfully guided the team, raised his public profile, and helped direct construction of the Rangers' new stadium, the Ballpark at Arlington. His father's defeat, as Rove said, now opened the door for George W. to enter the 1994 race for governor.

First thing, Bush had to learn about Texas government. He was well grounded in the gilded assumptions of country club Republicanism: taxes are bad, free enterprise is good, government that governs least, governs best. He was an attractive candidate, with his father's handsome features, piercing blue eyes, a thin, athletic build, and a bright smile. Bush knew almost nothing, however, about state government.

The machinery of Texas government was huge and sprawling, like the state itself. It regulated oil and eggs and the number of grade school students permitted in a classroom. Texas government oversaw fisheries on the Gulf Coast and seed corn programs in the Panhandle, administered the largest prison system in the free world, and limited how much sales tax big cities like Dallas and Houston could charge to operate mass transit. The state budget was $70 billion and growing, and the biggest portion went to public education. Much of state government was invisible to the average Texan, but voters knew their public schools and cared a great deal about education. They cared about crime, too. Those were two major issues in any governor's race, crime and education, and a key to beating Governor Ann Richards, was to prove she had done a bad job on both. To do that, Bush had to understand both issues as well as Richards did.

In early 1993, a few months after the elder Bush's loss, Rove called an Austin lobbyist named Mike Toomey and asked if he would go to Dallas and begin briefing Bush on state government and the budget. Toomey was the perfect pick for the role of tutor. He was knowledgeable and discreet, a former Republican member of the Texas House who had earned the nickname "Mike the Knife" for his conservative pursuit of budget cuts. Toomey was cowboy thin, with dark hair and dark eyes and a serious expression. There was no campaign at this point, only Rove and Toomey and a bundle of papers in a briefcase that Toomey carried as he flew to Dallas to meet Bush at the Texas Rangers' office along the expressway.

"I remember standing up there with charts on the budget," said Toomey. "It was early 1993. No one else was hired. This guy was just starting to call for money and it was the very beginning. Then they asked me, as the campaign was heating up, to put the policy together."

The tutoring sessions lasted for months. Teams flew to Dallas, and met with Bush in a small conference room, where they delivered a crash course on Texas civics. Bill Ratliff, a Republican state senator from East Texas and expert on school finance, flew up on two separate occasions for daylong sessions with Bush.

"He didn't know much," said Ratliff, who was chairman of the Senate Education Committee. "He knew that public schools were hidebound in too many regulations and needed to go to a more market-based approach. He didn't take notes that I remember."

Bush knew business, though, the oil business, the marketing of the Texas Rangers baseball team. He didn't have to be told that the state's franchise tax treated partnerships differently than corporations. He had a business-friendly aversion to government regulation and was instinctively suspicious of the claims of environmentalists. When his friend Ralph Wayne dispatched a team of three people from Austin to brief him on the effort to protect business from the growing number of injury lawsuits, they found in Bush a natural ally. Bush called Wayne to reassure him that he was preaching to the converted, although he couldn't resist a good-natured jibe over the makeup of the team. It included a lobbyist with close ties to Democrats, a top aide to the last Democratic governor, and the son of a former advisor to Lyndon Johnson.

"You sent me three Democrats to brief me on tort reform," Bush said. "If I run, you do know I'm going to run as a Republican?"

It wouldn't have bothered Rove that they were Democrats, because they weren't really Democrats at all—not in a way that would hamper Bush's chances. Texas had long ago divided itself into two parties, the conservative Democrats and the liberal Democrats. Business sided with the former to advance its agenda. Railroads, cattle, then oil and energy and construction—the business lobby in Texas had long cultivated conservative Democrats in positions of power. With the emergence of the Republican Party, business began gravitating to the GOP. For the first time since the Civil War, they needed to build ties with politicians who called themselves Republican.

The politics was simple enough: Since trial lawyers supported Democrats, business should support Republicans. Rove's work in the late 1980s helping to elect Republican judges to the Texas Supreme Court, starting with Tom Phillips, was only the beginning. Now, Rove worked fiendishly to steer business money to candidates—his candidates—all the way up the ballot. Trial lawyers were among the biggest source of campaign contributions to Democrats, including Ann Richards. Rove's task was to systematically direct business contributions to Republicans, especially George W. Bush.

One day in the office of the Texas Association of Business, a group of influential business executives gathered for a private meeting to talk about prospects of a race between Governor Ann Richards and George W. Bush. By almost any measure, Richards seemed unassailable. She was smart and funny, one of the most popular governors in Texas history. She had remade the boards and commissions that govern state agencies by appointing a record number of women and minorities. She had emerged as a national celebrity, the wisecracking governor who derided George W.'s father from the stage of the Democratic National Convention and thereby earned the enmity of the Bush family, especially George W., who relished the prospect of unseating Richards. The conventional wisdom was that beating the governor would be hard, maybe even impossible.

Not so, said Ralph Wayne, looking around the table at his colleagues. Wayne represented a confederation of tort-reform business interests called the Civil Justice League.

"Governor Richards can't win," he said. He explained that while Richards would have the backing of minority voters and organized labor, business would line up behind Bush. Wayne's assessment quickly reached the Richards camp. Not long afterwards, Richards had an announcement: She was establishing the Governor's Business Council, made up of some of the biggest corporate names in Texas and headed by Ken Lay, chief operating officer of Enron, who later became one of Bush's most significant fund-raisers in his first campaign for president.

Wayne called Rove to apologize, saying his remarks likely prompted the governor to act. Rove wasn't upset at all.

"Naah. She's not going to get any votes there."

What Rove knew, and Richards did not, was that Ken Lay and most of his business colleagues were firmly in the Bush camp. Rove knew Lay through the father. Ken Lay had been one of the elder Bush's biggest campaign contributors, co-host of the 1992 Republican National Convention in Houston, a long-time family friend. His was a name that bubbled to the top in every Rove campaign money list. Rove knew that Lay and Enron would have to give some money to Richards as the incumbent, but that their true interest was with Bush.

He was right. In the final accounting, state records show that Lay and Enron executives gave $146,500 to Bush, nearly seven times more than they did to Richards. Enron's political action committee and executives went on to become the largest donors to Bush's re-election and to his presidential campaign. And the rest of business would do the same.

In short order, they had an agenda: improve education, get tough on crime, reform welfare, and limit lawsuits against business.

Moreover, they had a detailed battle plan, which an aide recalled that Rove developed "like an artist in a burst of creativity."

"He would go into his office at 8 in the morning," said Toomey. "Shut the door, get on his Apple computer and work for 12 hours straight, then go get something to eat and come back. And it was like Karl would just download the plan into his head, tracking the whole campaign: In February, this is what you're going to do and where you're going to go, what you're going to say, the groups that are going to endorse you. Here's what you're going to do to the other guy.

"It was all laid out from January to October: Go back to East Texas eight times during this time period—not seven times, not 10 times—eight times. Karl is a big, big believer in having a scripted plan."

At campaign headquarters one day, Toomey noticed a set of books lining the wall. There was a large dictionary and a dense collection of volumes that Rove had given Bush over time. Myron Magnet's *The Dream and the Nightmare*, Marvin Olasky's *The Tragedy of American Compassion*, Gertrude Himmelfarb's *The Demoralization of Society*, James Q. Wilson's *The Moral Sense and on Character*.

Bush had always bristled at the pretensions of intellectualism. In 1988, he told author Doug Wead that he had always read more for entertainment than knowledge.

"I was never a great intellectual. I like books and pick them up and read them for the fun of it."

Rove was the reader; he was forever carrying around a heavy volume on history or political theory. Once, when a friend invited Rove to join him at a National Football League playoff game between the Dallas Cowboys and the San Francisco 49ers, Rove brought along a book about the Civil War, which he read between plays, during time outs and at half time.

Rove brought intellectual ballast to the collaboration, but was sensitive to the perception that Bush wasn't smart and he worked hard to promote his boss' image. Six months before Bush formally launched his campaign for the presidency, a story appeared in the

National Review about Bush and his prodigious reading habits. The source of the article was Rove.

"In addition to Magnet's book," the article said, "Bush has read and admired Wilson's *The Moral Sense and on Character*, Himmelfarb's *The Demoralization of Society*, and Olasky's *The Tragedy of American Compassion*."

This was Karl Rove's reading list. Not Bush's.

Not only that, according to the magazine, Bush had recently read Paul Johnson's mammoth *History of the American People* and that he "with Rove kept a running list of Johnson's minor mistakes."

In November 1993, Bush took his fledgling gubernatorial campaign to San Antonio, where he addressed a small group of school administrators. He delivered the message he and his policy team had developed: the state's education system under Ann Richards had suffered, teachers had too much paperwork and Texas' method of funding public schools needed to be changed.

After his speech, Bush wandered out into the richly ornate courtyard of the Menger Hotel adjacent to the Alamo. He moved with a kind of breezy confidence, smiling, shaking hands, and introducing himself to people getting their first look at the man who had chosen to challenge the vaunted Ann Richards.

A reporter from Austin approached and asked about his education plan. Bush resurrected some sentences from his speech, asserting that education was his top priority. When the reporter asked him a question about the workings of the state's education agency, apparently not in his briefing book, Bush stood for a moment, blinking.

He did not know the answer.

Exactly how would his plan change the school-finance formula? He didn't know.

How much would it cost?

Again, he demurred.

"Will voters know how much money would be involved before election?"

Bush shifted from foot to foot, his brain swimming.

"Probably not."

It was not an auspicious start. An early news conference with the Austin Capitol press corps proved nearly as bad with Bush stumbling over some of his answers.

"He was shaky and you guys sensed it," a Bush associate recalled. "Everything is confidence. And Bush is really transparent. He does not play act; he's a real direct guy who wears his emotions on his sleeve."

Heading for the campaign plane, Bush looked deflated. An aide offered some advice.

"Look, you are the son of a president. You've got an MBA from Harvard. You want to be governor. You can stand in front of these Capitol reporters for 20 minutes and take their questions, because if you can't, what are we doing?"

At campaign headquarters, Rove mapped a travel schedule that gave Bush more seasoning on the small-town Rotary circuit. For several months, Bush traveled to little communities where he introduced himself to business and civic groups, did radio interviews and learned to answer questions largely outside the glare of the media in Austin, Dallas, and Houston. His campaign travels took him to a mobile home lot in Navasota, Sadler's Bar-B-Que Sales in Henderson, the leather company in Yoakum, the wire works in Shiner. He shook hands at a community reception in the Hawkeye Hunting Club near Center; he walked down the main street of Stamford in the Cowboy Reunion Parade.

It was a brilliant piece of political engineering. By summer, Bush was a better candidate, well-prepared and well-positioned to face Ann Richards in the fall. The race for governor was to be the showroom where Karl Rove displayed his product; the man he was grooming to be the next president of the United States.

10

To the Victor

Life in the twentieth century is like a parachute jump: you have
to get it right the first time.

—Margaret Mead

The landscape of West Texas lies as flat as a billiard table, un-
adorned but for a tangle of desert scrub and the bobbing
heads of tireless pump jacks pulling oil from the ground.
Oil has been the business of Midland since 1923, when a
rig called Santa Rita #1 hit the first big strike 60 miles southeast of
town in what is known as the Permian Basin. Midland had been a
farm town before that, just a brief stopping point along the Texas &
Pacific Railway that crossed the unceasing distances of the American
West. When the Santa Rita blew, everything changed. As it turned
out, Midland and its sister city Odessa were on top of the largest
concentration of oil ever found in the continental United States.

Oil made millionaires of a whole group of rugged West Texas
gamblers, including John Cox, who had made a fortune and lost a
fortune and made it back again in the roller-coaster economies of
black gold. He was one of the Midland Eight. When Forbes magazine ran its first list of the wealthiest people in America in 1982,

eight were from Midland, with its modest population of 80,000, and Cox was one of them.

In early December 1990, Ann Richards traveled to Midland to see John Cox, and she brought with her Lena Guerrero. The day before, Richards had named Guerrero to the Texas Railroad Commission, the first major appointment of her new administration. Guerrero was a 33-year-old state representative from Austin, dark-haired, attractive, and politically shrewd. She represented everything Ann Richards wanted to say about opening the doors of opportunity—a young Hispanic woman, a former migrant farm worker in the Rio Grande Valley, a rising political star in a New Texas where "men and woman, and white, black and brown alike are going to be in positions of power and responsibility in this state."

"I want the appointment of Lena to send a message to the people of Texas," Richards told the crowd in the Senate chamber.

The Texas Railroad Commission regulates oil and gas production, and Guerrero seemed an unlikely choice for the job. She had no experience in the energy business. She was an unabashed political liberal whose district included Austin's barrio and modest working-class neighborhoods on the city's East Side.

The next morning, Richards and Guerrero flew to Midland to see John Cox, who had read about the appointment in the local newspaper. Cox was 65, a plainspoken petroleum engineer with a lifetime of experience drilling dry holes and gushers in the fickle moonscape of the Permian Basin. The first thing that struck him was how young Guerrero was and how inexperienced. And that she was a woman. Guerrero was the first female member of the Texas Railroad Commission in its 100 years of existence.

He looked at the front page of the Midland paper, then at the young Hispanic woman with jet-black hair, standing before him in a neat business suit.

"Forget about environmental issues and trying to get jobs in Mexico. Your job is going to be railroad commissioner."

Guerrero nodded. "Give me a chance," she said, "and take me to an oil field."

Lena Guerrero was the next big thing in Texas, a young, bright, Ann Richards-in-waiting. Even the Texas governor agreed.

"I have very high hopes for her future."

Because her appointment was to an unexpired term, Guerrero had to stand for election in 1992. She was the prohibitive favorite. Although Republicans had begun to win a few offices, the state remained largely Democrat. Guerrero was the incumbent and she had the exuberant backing of Ann Richards, a national celebrity whose popularity back home was among the highest ever for a governor in the state's long-standing survey, the Texas Poll.

Karl Rove, and almost Rove alone, was confident that Richards could be beaten in 1994 and that George W. Bush was the candidate to do it. But in developing a plan to make Bush governor, his actions demonstrated a belief that he needed to go beyond simply unseating Richards after one term. He would have to stop future Democratic stars. And more—he would take great pains to discredit, eliminate, and damage those associated with Richards.

The evidence of subsequent events makes it clear that Rove took steps to eliminate the Richards network of political friends and allies, undercutting their performance in state jobs and damaging their careers in the private sector. Every vestige of Ann Richards had to be eliminated if the Republican Party was to triumph in Texas.

First, though, Rove had to stop Lena Guerrero.

Rove's client in the race against Guerrero was Barry Williamson, an affable energy lawyer from Midland with soft features and a tousle of brown hair who had served in Energy Department posts in the Reagan and Bush administrations. Nobody had ever heard of Barry Williamson, at least nobody outside a small circle of oil industry types and members of the Bush family. Williamson, however, had none of Guerrero's political sparkle.

In July, Rove produced a mass mailing for voters that described Guerrero as soft on crime, pro-gay rights, antigun, and an enemy of traditional family values. But as Election Day approached, Guerrero was still leading in the polls and, with Richards' help, was raising more in campaign contributions than her Republican opponent.

"We needed to do something to cut off her money," Rove later told a reporter.

One piece of information in Rove's possession just might do the trick. From a fellow Republican with ties to the University of Texas, Rove learned that although Guerrero claimed on her campaign resume to be a graduate of the University of Texas, school records indicated she had never graduated. Rove picked up the phone and called a newspaper reporter with the information.

Even Rove hadn't anticipated how badly she would botch the response.

Guerrero initially denied it, but a day later issued a statement acknowledging that she had only recently learned that she was four hours short of a college degree. The story hit Saturday's newspapers. Guerrero's campaign hurriedly called a news conference for Sunday.

The press turned out in force for the news conference that afternoon at the downtown Marriott. Television crews erected a battery of cameras pointed, like guns, at Guerrero, her husband, her 4-year-old son, and her mother. She told reporters that she mistakenly thought she had graduated from college and that she had never noticed that her news releases over the years erroneously claimed she was a member of Phi Beta Kappa.

"Nobody's going to believe this story," Richards media man Chuck McDonald told the governor.

And nobody did, certainly not Rove, who began circulating every press release Guerrero had ever issued, every biography, as if to cast doubt on everything she had ever said. He urged reporters to demand her college transcripts, which she released out of fear that Rove would somehow get them anyway—and that spawned a new round of stories because Guerrero actually was far more than four hours short of graduation. Every new revelation produced a new story. Every story reinforced the theme that Rove advanced like a drum beat with reporters—Lena Guerrero can't be trusted to tell the truth.

Shortly after the initial story broke, Republican Barry Williamson was on a campaign swing in East Texas. He dropped by a small diner in Navasota and moved from table to table, shaking hands and introducing himself as a candidate for the Railroad Commission and asking people for their vote. A man looked up from his chicken-fried steak.

"I have one question for you," he said. "Did you graduate from college?"

Williamson smiled. "I knew we had won. If that man in that town had figured this out, I knew this race was ours."

A vanity photo of candidate Guerrero sitting smartly on an oil well valve made the cover of *Texas Monthly* magazine just before the election, but with a screaming two-word headline: "Lena's Lies." Guerrero lost in a landslide by 845,000 votes.

"I think that was the beginning of the end for Ann Richards when they blew up Lena Guerrero," McDonald said.

The effort to damage two political confidants of Ann Richards was something else entirely. Jane Hickie directed the state's office in Washington; assisting the Texas congressional delegation and representing the interests of state officials back home. Cathy Bonner headed the Texas Department of Commerce for three years before returning to her public relations business. Both were long-time Richards' friends, instrumental in her election in 1990, and both returned to help direct the reelection. The assault on Guerrero was on the party's future. The attack on them was an attack on the party's present star, Ann Richards; even before her reelection campaign was fully underway.

Hickie was scrupulous in her operations of the Office of State-Federal Relations in Washington. She kept detailed records, a strict schedule, and she always made certain to clear everything with both Democrats and Republicans in the state's congressional delegation. If Republican Representative Dick Armey didn't want something included on the state office's agenda of things to do, it was scratched. If Republican Senator Kay Bailey Hutchison wanted something added to the list, it was added. Hickie worked to make the office as nonpartisan as possible, even retaining some young Republicans on staff from the previous administration. Her predecessor in Washington was a gifted political operator whose convivial style led to lavish entertainment of lawmakers and lobbyists well into the night with alcohol and good cigars. Hickie's approach was decidedly more businesslike.

Rove still had Bush on the small-town circuit when stories began appearing in the Houston Post questioning the finances of the state's Washington office. First there were stories about expenditures at the state office, then about whether political fund-raising was happening on state time. Some phone records back in Austin had been destroyed, prompting a new round of stories. Outraged over the "ethical lapses," the Bush for Governor Campaign issued a statement recalling the Guerrero debacle and then denouncing Hickie and operations of the state's office in Washington.

"First, there was political work being done in that government office. Then, public documents were destroyed to cover it up. Now, we have evidence of further misuse of taxpayer dollars by Ms. Hickie."

At the State-Federal office in Washington, Hickie gathered telephone records, press releases, and receipts, and called a news conference. She showed that the office finances had actually saved the state money and that there was no political fund-raising in the office. In the end, the flurry of news stories had led to little evidence of wrongdoing, but the damage had been done. Questions had been raised publicly about a Richards operative in Washington mixing government and politics.

The issue of doing political business on state time was fresh in Rove's mind. A year earlier, Rove had defended one of his own clients against exactly the same charge. Kay Bailey Hutchison, newly elected to the U.S. Senate, was indicted by a Travis County grand jury in September 1993 on charges she misused her office as state treasurer. Specifically, prosecutors said workers on her payroll made campaign fund-raising calls on state time and used a state computer to keep track of contributions.

Republicans launched an assault on District Attorney Ronnie Earle's credibility, orchestrated by Rove. As Hutchison rode in the back of a van to the courthouse where the grand jury was meeting, Rove was on the cell phone reassuring her.

"He was constantly with the candidate and had people around her stay on the attack—either an attack on Ronnie Earle or a total denial of the charges," said an associate.

Attorneys for Hutchison were desperate to advance the idea that the district attorney was a publicity-hungry politico looking to higher office. Their best evidence was their insistence that reporters had been tipped in advance—assuring maximum publicity—of a raid on Hutchison's treasury office to rescue records. It was not true, but Rove took the stand in court and said it was.

"Do you have information about whether reporters were notified in advance about the June 10th Treasury raid?" defense lawyer Dick Deguerin asked Rove at a pretrial hearing.

"Yes."

Rove testified that he got a call from the *Dallas Morning News*. It was not true. In fact, The News did not get advance word, but learned about the raid from one of Hutchison's employees after it was well underway. Rove testified that an Austin newspaper reporter, David Elliott, had been tipped in advance.

Not true, Elliott said years later. Elliott, like other reporters, got word of the raid long after it had begun.

"I specifically remember them telling me that the treasurer's office was being raided. It was not anything like advance knowledge. That, I'm absolutely certain."

Rove's testimony, however, reinforced the thesis: the district attorney was a publicity-hungry politico. The case never went to trial. The judge dismissed evidence important to prosecutors, the district attorney dropped the case, and Hutchison took her place in the U.S. Senate.

"They mounted a political defense," said Earle. "They wanted to portray the entire effort as a political prosecution. They played that defense both in the courtroom and outside. Their courtroom tactics and their public relations tactics were the same."

In a political endnote, the state Republican Party issued a news release saying the district attorney's time would better be spent investigating Ann Richards. Whatever else Rove was doing, he never lost sight of his primary goal: putting George W. Bush in office. Richards was the obstacle; Richards was the enemy. The news release came two months before Bush formally announced his candidacy and was written by Karen Hughes, who eventually was to join Rove on the Bush political team.

Like Jane Hickie, Cathy Bonner found herself the subject of unfavorable publicity generated by Rove as part of the campaign against Ann Richards. Bonner resigned from the Texas Department of Commerce and returned to private business in order to join the Richards' 1994 reelection effort. Rove targeted her for years. His political investigators sought out information about her business, which Rove tried to get reporters to write. When her old firm got a state contract from the Texas Education Agency, stories questioning the deal popped up in Texas newspapers.

"The fact that he comes after you and tries to ruin you professionally is kind of bizarre," said Bonner.

Rove did not limit his aim exclusively to Democrats. He targeted Republicans as well, those who might challenge him professionally. Democrats were political opponents; Republicans could be professional rivals. There's a political cliché that each side wants a level playing field. In Rove's case, it appeared as if he wanted to level everything on the playing field.

Bill Miller, a veteran consultant who represented business and political clients, said Rove is one of the most compelling and accomplished allies—and enemies—he's ever met. Miller teamed with Rove in a Texas Senate race in the early 1990s. Miller handled the phone banks and Rove was directing the mass mail operation. The candidate called one day and wanted a status report.

"I do my deal, pretty straight forward," said Miller, who then watched in awe as Rove offered a presentation so elaborate and thorough he was mesmerized.

"Karl had the entire history of the campaign, the history of the earth from day one. It is a huge, wonderful presentation—way beyond the scope of what was asked for, but it's a tour de force. And I sat there and thought, if there ever was a doubt, if there ever was a question about who really is always going to get the upper hand in everything, he won the game today."

John Weaver was one of Rove's best friends and became his most bitter rival. Weaver was a tall, laconic figure, deeply introspective. Rove was a careening burst of energy. But they both shared a brilliant instinct for politics and considered forming a single company until small frictions began to develop and it became clear that Rove did not want competition. Rove worked harder, longer, and undercut Weaver in Texas, then discouraged other candidates nationally from hiring him.

In the 2000 presidential race, they met in the biggest showdown of all—Rove directing Bush's effort and Weaver advising maverick Republican John McCain. Again, Rove won and he pursued Weaver even from the White House, where word reached potential business clients not to hire his old political enemy.

Eventually, Weaver left the party entirely and took a job advising Democrats.

Rove simply worked harder than anyone else, harder and longer, driven by some internal need to tackle 100 things at once in pursuit of the single goal: making George W. Bush the most powerful political figure on earth, and lifting himself in the process. As the architect of Bush's political fortunes, Rove was obsessive about protecting their relationship; a collaboration he was convinced would lead to the White House. He jealously guarded his proximity to Bush and was forever blocking others from getting too close.

As he traveled the Rotary circuit according to Rove's script, Bush privately had doubts whether he could beat Ann Richards. The showy confidence he reflected during his tutorials early on had dimmed. Richards seemed too strong, too popular. But Rove never stopped reassuring him that he would win. Rove hauled out charts and graphs and repeated his elaborate thesis that Richards could not withstand the right challenge from the right candidate, and Bush was that candidate.

"For a while, he was just afraid. He didn't want to get beat so badly he would embarrass the legacy of his father," said a campaign aide. "But by September, he began to think he could win."

Bush was watching television one day when he saw a Richards' commercial in which her white hair was lost in the white background.

"There's something wrong with that campaign," Bush said. "Somebody's not paying attention."

As he climbed aboard the campaign plane with a couple of aides in the heat of late summer, Bush was having trouble reconciling his opponent's powerful persona and the fact that she was running a lackluster campaign. He had always feared that Richards would simply switch on the jets and win, but it wasn't happening.

"Is this all there is?" he asked no one in particular, buckling his seat belt. "I thought she was this great politician. But she's not doing a damn thing."

Bush looked out the window at the familiar stretch of tarmac and the line of live oaks on the horizon. Maybe Rove was right.

"I'm going to win this goddamn thing."

11

Contests without Rules

A rumor without a leg to stand on will get around some other way.
—John Tudor

Outside the Loews Anatole Hotel, a glittering line of Mercedes and Cadillacs and steel-grey Lincoln Town Cars reflected the glory that is Dallas. Inside the ballroom, the television lights blazed. And in the halo of television lights, accepting the applause of the crowd, newly elected U.S. Senator Kay Bailey Hutchison positively beamed as she stood on stage.

"I will be a senator for all of Texas. All of us want our country to get back on track," she said into the cheers of the Republican throng.

In winning the special election for the Senate in June 1993, Hutchison toppled Governor Ann Richards' hand-picked Democratic candidate, giving the Republican Party both seats in the U.S. Senate for the first time since 1875. Her colleague, Senator Phil Gramm, stood with her on stage, as did a retinue of Republicans of importance and semi-importance, among them the managing general partner of the Texas Rangers baseball team, George W. Bush, who on this night was just another face in the crowd.

This night belonged to Hutchison. She had followed the blueprint of her consultant, Karl Rove, and crushed her opponent by a margin of 2–1. She was the newest, brightest star in a Rove constellation that was overtaking politics in the Lone Star State. At the Anatole, the Republicans were giddy with victory. Music boomed over the loudspeaker and Hutchison's campaign manager, Brian Berry, worked his way around the ballroom in a burst of adrenaline that masks fatigue on election nights.

Karl Rove came bounding down from the stage and, spotting Berry, poked him on the shoulder.

"Hey, buddy. Are you ready for another one?"

Berry seemed confused.

"We might have some plans here," Rove said.

Even in the hoopla of this election night, Rove was already at work on the next campaign—the big one this time, the campaign to put George W. Bush in the Governor's Mansion. And he wanted Berry on the team. Berry was a veteran campaign operative, bright and impulsive, with long, skinny limbs, red hair, and a commitment to the Young Republican school of smash-mouth politics. Rove had cleared the way for Berry to head the Southwest region for President Bush's reelection race in 1992, had picked him to direct Hutchison's Senate campaign. Berry was part of a growing Rove team, an ensemble cast of political players inserted into the various roles in various campaigns—but there was never any doubt who the director was, who was serving as the production's impresario.

"This is the way Karl works. He always is into personnel. Personnel is power," said Berry.

To produce the campaign's television commercials, Rove's choice was Don Sipple, a California media whiz and master of the 30-second sound bite. Sipple and Rove worked together on campaigns for John Ashcroft of Missouri, first for governor, then senator. Sipple's presentation was dazzling, impressive; exactly what Bush was looking for, exactly what Rove wanted. Bush and Sipple met for three hours, one-on-one, just the two of them, and in the end Sipple came away with the job and with a deep impression about Bush the candi-

date. First, were Bush's eyes, which had a kind of brittle blue intensity that were perfect for a commercial.

"He looked at me with those steely blue eyes and I said, 'Holy shit.'"

Second, Sipple was struck by Bush's pledge not to go negative
against Ann Richards. Bush said Richards' record was fair game, but
he would not go after her personally.

In fact, the campaign against Richards was to be negative, harsh,
and very personal. There actually were two campaigns against
Richards, one in which Bush floated above the fray and another in
which Rove targeted the Democrat's politics and gender. It was an
arrangement that allowed Bush plausible deniability, no matter
what. And it was a model of future Bush races: Bush traveling the
high road, Rove pursuing the low. Rove's strategy in the Richards'
race was simple enough: Bush the candidate engages his Democratic
opponent by respectfully challenging her record on improving public schools and fighting crime. Meanwhile, Bush surrogates, operating at arm's length, undermine Richards on the issues of guns and
gays, including a vicious whisper campaign about lesbianism that
ran with an evangelical fervor through the coffee shops and church
parlors of East Texas. Rove used this blueprint again and again in
campaigns against John McCain, John Kerry, and every senate and
congressional campaign he conducted.

Richards made a national splash at the 1988 Democratic Convention when she took aim at Bush's father and delivered the line
heard around the political world: "Poor George, he can't help
it . . . he was born with a silver foot in his mouth." The remark
struck a deep nerve with the family. Barbara Bush, watching on television while on retreat at Kennebunkport, let it be known the comment made her physically sick. In a single phrase, Richards had
highlighted the twin weaknesses of the Bush clan politically, attacking it as both ardently patrician and vaguely ineffective.

The image of Ann Richards in her luminescent blue dress and
white hair, standing on the podium in Atlanta, cheerfully delivering
that attack on his father, left Bush . . . steaming, and he could not
forget it, would not forget, as he made clear in the private confines of

his office where he spoke of Richards with contempt. Bush listed her among the cabal that contributed to his father's defeat, Ann Richards and Bill Clinton and all the GOP traitors who he felt were more interested in protecting themselves than serving his father in the final days, men like Jim Baker III and other lower-level Republican toadies—these were who Bush blamed for his father's humiliating loss.

Bush harbored his father's loss like a wound. Nobody understood Bush's visceral desire to redeem the family name better than Rove, who acted as a kind of political Bundini, constantly assuring that for all her popularity, Richards was vulnerable politically and could be beaten.

"They like her hair, but they're not strongly anchored to her," he said.

Rove was the picture of confidence, but in the beginning Bush believed the news clippings about the glib and gifted Ann Richards, political superstar.

Self-doubt was not a suit that Rove wore.

As always, he found substantiation in the numbers. He studied immigration patterns and voter rolls, the bursting growth in the suburbs north of Dallas and around Houston, the blooming high-tech industry, the shifting election trends in which the voters of Texas— once stalwart Southern Democrats in the Roosevelt tradition—were increasingly identifying themselves as independents and Republicans. Private polls intimated at the positive prospects of a candidate like Bush, but the first public head-to-head survey, the Texas Poll published in state newspapers in October 1993, was a revelation. It had Richards at 47 percent and Bush at 39 percent. Richards had been governor for three years, Bush had never served a day in office, and in their first poll, Bush was only trailing by eight points. Eight points! And Bush hadn't even announced yet.

If the father and the father's name was a strength, Rove knew also it was a weakness, especially in Texas where the notion of dynasty carried with it the nasty connotation of the Kennedys. Bush would have to answer the question: What have you done?

"He knew what the Democrats would do, that they would tag George W. as the son of George Bush, as somebody trying to trade on your father's name. And from that, Karl developed a policy to trump Richards by not engaging on that turf. We had a standard line: I love my father. That was George W.'s line. Every time they said, 'Aren't you trading on your father's name?' he said, 'I love my father.'"

Though father and son talked frequently, the decision was made to keep George Bush largely out of sight, except for a pair of fund-raisers in Dallas and Houston where the ex-president joined his son but did not speak. His first campaign finance report was top-heavy with contributions from his father's biggest donors. The strategy—Rove's strategy—was to reap the advantages of being a president's son while minimizing the problems.

"Here you have a businessman, manager of the Texas Rangers, a popular sport," said Berry. "You can show your charismatic side, but you also show your business side, that you're not a pol. You can have the separation from your father just on the basis of that, that you're running your own gig."

This was hardly a newfound thought for Bush.

His foray into business had largely been a flop, characterized mostly by a series of takeover deals in which outside investors with ties to his father periodically swooped in to save one foundering oil company after another. Arbusto Energy became Bush Exploration, which merged with Spectrum 7, which merged with Harken Energy. And while the companies were losing money because of depressed oil prices, Bush's equity increased in value until 1990 when he sold 212,000 shares of Harken stock for $848,560 to pay off his investment in the Texas Ranger baseball team. By 1993, when Bush was preparing his race for governor, the major league ball team had become a smashing success with a bright new stadium and a devoted fan base in the community.

Construction of the new ballpark in Arlington was subsidized by an increase in the sales tax in the team's home city of Arlington. In the public campaign to promote the sales tax hike, Bush remained prudently out of sight. Otherwise, in operations at the team's old ballpark, Arlington Stadium, and association with the new field with its red-brick retro design, Bush was very much the front man, the president's son as pitch man. "I like selling tickets," he told a reporter for Time magazine.

The political potential of the baseball deal was not lost on Bush. A month after closing the deal to buy the team in 1989 in which Bush helped assemble the consortium of investors, a reporter asked whether purchase of the Rangers might portend some future political plans.

He didn't even blink. "This job has a very high visibility, which cures the political problem I'd have: 'What has the boy done?'"

In promoting Bush as a potential candidate for governor, Rove told a newspaper reporter: "Ownership of the Texas Rangers anchors him clearly as a Texas businessman and entrepreneur and gives him name identification, exposure and gives him something that will be easily recallable by people."

But it was Bush's role in running the club, his business acumen, that Rove pushed in the campaign's early months. Bush was a businessman; Richards was not. He was the linchpin that made the transaction happen. So when a reporter asked about details of the Ranger deal, Bush appeared ready with answers.

"Am I going to benefit off it financially? I hope so," he said. "But I also hope that the $100 million that comes into Arlington will help Arlington schools and helps Arlington streets and police. And I hope Arlington becomes the finest city in the Metroplex."

Bush and partner Tom Schieffer fielded questions together, questions about the annual rent, land condemnation, future ownership of the property. Then the phone rang in Schieffer's office and he left to take the call. Bush sat alone now and the reporter asked about the seat bond program. Why was it that fans were being asked to front the club money—ranging in price from $500 to $5,000, with discounts for longtime season ticket holders—to purchase season tickets in the new park?

Bush turned and looked in the direction of Schieffer's office, but his partner was still on the phone. Bush hazarded an answer, but it was incomplete. Clearly, he did not fully understand the deal even though his campaign was trumpeting his management of the Rangers as evidence of his business skills. Bush turned again, looking anxiously for Schieffer.

"Let's wait until Tom gets back," he said.

Schieffer did know the answer.

The bonds were an "interest-free loan" from the fans to the Rangers. The fans would be repaid over time from a $1 surcharge levied on each Ranger ticket, but the team would pocket the interest. In lieu of interest, Schieffer said, fans got the right to buy preferential seating. But if Bush appeared lost in the financial minutiae of his company's tax breaks and interest-free loans, Rove knew it didn't matter. What did matter was that Bush was a businessman with a name and political pedigree that guaranteed money and attention. Moreover, the very public campaign against Richards was turning on issues the people of Texas cared about, especially education and crime.

"The sense was that she was popular but had no real achievements," Rove said years later in an interview recalling the campaign's early days. "The state faced a problem of leadership in that the people wanted somebody to do something, whether it was education, which was the No. 1 issue, or whether it was crime, particularly where we faced this generation of juvenile criminals."

Rove understood what many of the early campaign staffers did not, that Bush was not only a country-club Republican—lower taxes, less regulation—but also a social conservative in a way his father was not. Bush disliked the openness and lassitude of the 1960s. He felt a generation had been damaged by a counterculture philosophy of "if it feels good, do it"—a line he was to use repeatedly in his race for governor and, later, in his campaign for the presidency. Rove suggested he talk to Marvin Olasky, a University of Texas professor who had just written a book skewering the liberal approach of the welfare state, *The Tragedy of American Compassion*. In Olasky's view, nineteenth-century America's religious-based charity was a better model for dealing with the poor, not the hoary apparatus of the War on Poverty in which public assistance had become a matter of entitlement, squeezing out personal responsibility—just goo-goo social policy that delivered a state-sanctioned subsistence and asked nothing in return. Bush called Olasky and suggested they meet.

Olasky was a small man with a thin face, a close-cropped beard, and large eyes that never seemed to blink. He had a bird-like quality, as if forever looking sideways at an object. He was a communist turned atheist turned evangelical Christian who burned with the conviction of a convert. Unlike some professional moralists, Olasky lived his faith; he and his wife adopted a Black child who needed a home, worked in soup kitchens, assisted ex-cons in need of a second chance. He believed deeply in helping the poor and Bush came away from their discussion won over by Olasky's view that the missing element in the current welfare state was spiritual rather than material. The program's problem was that it didn't promote values.

"The two issues, education and juvenile justice, were on his agenda list. And they were on the people's agenda list," said Rove. "Now, welfare was not, the idea of the compassionate conservative, faith-based institutions—that was not on their radar scope in a public way, but it was on Bush's. Later, we added tort reform. I sort of talked him into that one."

Tort reform, the effort to shield businesses from rising jury awards in personal-injury lawsuits, was standard Republican boilerplate, but Rove wanted that issue elevated. Although he would never admit it, he had to know that its most ardent advocates in Texas could provide millions of dollars in campaign contributions needed to unseat Richards. Rove was a paid consultant to Philip Morris, which faced enormous liability problems, and over the years he had depended on the deep pockets of business—uber-givers like Houston builder Bob Perry, Enron's Ken Lay, East Texas chicken processor Lonnie "Bo" Pilgrim— to elect candidates who would be good for business.

Rove had the money lists. He had organized the early tutoring sessions, assembled the issue-development teams. He had put Bush early on the small-town circuit. ("Limit GWB's public appearance" in Austin "to reduce the attention of the Capitol press corps," he wrote in an October 1993 memo.) But when the campaign's senior staff gathered, Bush wanted it known that he—not Rove—framed the agenda of his campaign. At the meetings, Bush was clearly in command.

"When you're developing things," Bush said one day, looking around the table, "I'm going to tell you what I believe. You guys are the wordsmiths. You can smith it out. But it's going to start with what I think."

Everyone nodded, Rove included. There was a curious dance between the candidate and the consultant in which Rove clearly sought to steer Bush in a particular direction and Bush periodically would jerk the reins and reassert his authority. Early on, Bush was sensitive of being perceived a lightweight and Rove his Svengali.

"Bush puts down a marker and says don't get too much into my world, don't try to over-manage me," said Berry. "Rove is trying to work out the best avenue to take so he's not blamed for being the puppeteer. Bush repelled from that."

When Bush fumbled criticism of Richards over the destruction of state phone records, Rove sought to instruct his charge on doing a better job in the future—only to be cut short by a stern rebuke on the other end of the phone.

"I got confused," said Rove, suddenly backpedaling. "You did great."

Their odd rivalry, prickly and contentious at times, continued after Bush became governor. After a news conference one day on the lawn of the Governor's Mansion, Bush began walking back inside when he noticed reporters were clustered around Rove, continuing to ask questions. Bush stopped.

"Is the Rove news conference about over?" he asked in an irritated voice.

Rove blanched, turned abruptly, fled the circle of reporters, and followed the governor back into the mansion.

Whatever the impression of some Democrats outside the campaign—that Bush was a lightweight and Rove was at master control—those inside the campaign knew that something more complicated was going on. Bush was very much the chief executive, distilling information, evaluating proposals, pushing and prodding advisors to defend their positions.

Crime was a perfect issue.

Houston television stations, locked in a ratings war, were broadcasting hysterical reports nightly on every rape, every shooting as if the city were under siege. Even in Austin and Dallas, where news reports were more tempered, people were worried about crime.

Rove knew Texans were worried; polls showed it. Polls also showed that voters had more confidence in men than women when it came to fighting crime and protecting the rights of gun-owners. The fact that Richards had a good record on crime during her tenure as governor—violent crime was falling and she was responsible for the largest prison-building program in state history—seemed unimportant. In fact, it was irrelevant.

Rove's thesis was this: In designing a media message, you must build on what the public already believes. The public believes that women are softer on crime than men, especially women who are Democrats. And most especially, liberal women Democrats. So a media strategy was born to present Richards as soft on crime. She immediately would be on the defensive and respond with arguments and statistics showing otherwise, but it didn't matter.

Explaining is losing.

The true course of a winning campaign is just as Rove set out in his 1985 memo: Attack, Attack, Attack.

Sipple's clients in the 1994 race included Bush and two incumbent Republican governors, Pete Wilson in California and Jim Edgar in Illinois. All three were facing female opponents and in all three contests. Sipple produced virtually identical ads on crime. He even used the same black-and-white footage of a staged abduction and asserted the same promise to get tough on "rapists and child molesters." In a solemn voice, an announcer says: "Crime—more random, more violent. Incredibly, Ann Richards says she's reduced crime and violence in Texas."

Official state crime statistics showed the rate of violent crime in almost every category had topped out the year Richards took office and had fallen every year since, except for juvenile crime, which was up 52 percent. If the law-abiding burghers in the suburbs were concerned about crime in general, they were terrified at the prospect of violent young thugs with guns, stealing cars, committing murder.

"Crime is crime is crime," said Sipple. "But the campaign found one piece of the crime issue that was new, which I thought was genius. Juvenile crime was a way to open up a new front on the crime issue and it worked very well."

Rove had studied the voter trends in 1990, how the moderate suburban women flocked to Richards. Bush needed to win those voters back, and Rove was convinced the best way to do that was to maintain a respectful tone—criticize Richards' stewardship of state government, but never Richards personally.

"Here's what I'll do and here's what I won't do," Bush said, outlining the policy at an early campaign staff meeting. "On the attacking thing, I'm not doing this bit where we're tearing down. I'm not doing this same old kind of stuff. If that causes me to go in the ringer, that's fine. But I'm not going that route."

The campaign even institutionalized the notion with a 30-second television spot called "Personal." In the spring 1994, Bush and Sipple were filming a set of positive television commercials at a school. The night before, Sipple had scribbled an idea on a yellow pad about how Bush could protect himself from anticipated attacks by the Richards camp. The idea was for Bush to film a commercial in advance expressing disappointment that his Democratic opponent had decided to abandon the usual political discourse and launch personal attacks.

"We can put it in the can so we have it in case we need it," Sipple said.

Sipple sat Bush in a chair with a soft, golden light across his face. Bush looked directly into the camera and spoke in slow, measured tones.

"I have said all along I'm going to treat Governor Richards with respect, that my campaign would focus on the issues, the facts and the record," Bush said. "For whatever reasons, the governor has chosen to attack me personally."

Sipple was delighted. "We hit the seams just right with that one. I don't think I've ever seen anybody deliver something as well as he did. I remember he was quite enamored with it."

As the campaign moved into the summer, Bush traveled the state in accordance with Rove's methodical blueprint, complaining that schoolteachers were burdened by too much paperwork and that the state's accountability system of testing students needed to be strengthened. He said crime was up and promised to halt the early release of felons from prison. He challenged Richards' handling of welfare, questioned whether she'd done enough to promote jobs. Internal polling, which Rove pored over as if it were sacred script, indicated Bush was gaining ground. Richards found herself increasingly irritated by her opponent's assaults on her record.

"You just work like a dog, do well and all of a sudden, you've got some jerk who's running for public office telling everybody it's all a sham and it isn't real," she told a crowd in the sweltering August heat of Texarkana.

Bingo! The Bush campaign rushed its prepared spot onto the air. On televisions all across Texas, people saw the Republican candidate sitting solemnly, looking directly into the camera with the sad knowledge that his opponent had crossed the line.

"For whatever reason, the governor has chosen to attack me personally. . . ."

Ann Richards sat in the confines of her campaign plane, cruising just above the clouds. Below was the tawny patchwork of East Texas, once the rugged heart of yellow-dog Democrat country, now a region very much in play. She knew the place: the small town squares, the deep thickets of loblolly pine, the huge neon sign above the Swinnytown Baptist Church that declared in a blazing blue light: "A Going Church for a Coming Lord." Richards had won East Texas four years ago, wooing the region's conservative Democrats. But her appeal was very much in jeopardy this time because a dark whisper campaign was underway, maddeningly decentralized but marvelously effective.

"You have been hearing a very skillfully crafted Republican message," Richards said. "We confronted it first in East Texas in the spring."

"What message?" the single reporter on the plane asked.

She hesitated, "I know what it is, but I don't want to say."

It was virtually impossible in the summer of 1994 to get a haircut in East Texas or visit a coffee shop or go to church Wednesday nights without hearing about Ann Richards and the lesbians. It was a mean and virulent whisper campaign, born, as such things are, by a small fragment of fact. One of the main powers of a governor is to appoint thousands of people to the boards and commissions that operate government, and Richards had opened that process to record numbers of women, Blacks, and Hispanics. With Richards naming so many women and with her liberal social politics anathema in some quarters of East Texas, word spread that the governor was filling state government with lesbians. The truth was that some of her appointees were gay, including a high-profile appointment to the agency regulating utilities that created a buzz when the Lesbian/Gay Rights Lobby of Texas said the selection of "an 'out' lesbian to such a powerful commission gives our community something to celebrate."

Rove knew that Richards' appointees were a ripe target for attack. He enlisted business groups and conservative religious organizations to raise questions about their professional experience and qualifications. Bush set the issue in motion a full year before the election, cautioning that his opponent's appointees "have been people who have had agendas that may have been personal in nature." The code word was "personal." Nobody mentioned sexual orientation; they didn't need to.

"There was clearly an organized Republican movement to keep out there a couple of issues, gays and guns, in the forefront," said Chuck McDonald, who was Richards' press secretary. "And I don't think it's any secret that the person who really set the Republican agenda was Karl Rove. He drove it."

Rove's direct-mail firm produced a campaign brochure for distribution across East Texas attacking Richards for vetoing a bill to allow people to carry concealed handguns. But if Rove was driving the debate on Richards and homosexuality, he left few fingerprints. He professed no involvement whatsoever. Bush, he was quick to remind everyone, was committed to a positive campaign with no personal attacks.

But the matter was moving just the same, from courthouse to coffee shop, with a quiet efficiency along an informal network of Bush surrogates. So as Richards traveled in her campaign plane high above East Texas in August, she faced a dilemma. Ignoring the whisper campaign, which by now had metastasized into lurid gossip, didn't protect her from its damage. But talking about it legitimized the subject. She decided that if the Bush campaign wanted to put gays in her administration on the front page, it would have to do so itself.

A few days later, it did.

Bush's East Texas campaign chairman, state Senator Bill Ratliff, told reporters for the *Houston Post* that Richards' appointment of homosexuals could cost her support in the region. "It is simply part of their culture, and frankly part of mine, that (homosexuality) is not something we encourage, reward, or acknowledge as an acceptable situation."

Richards' press secretary, Chuck McDonald, woke up to a storm of headlines. "The whisper campaign had come to life," he said.

The Bush campaign issued a news release praising the senator as a man "of great integrity and strong convictions," but said the

Republican candidate was running a positive campaign about the issues of education, juvenile crime, and welfare reform. "This is not an issue in this campaign." But the issue had been catapulted onto the front page of every newspaper in the state and the damage done. In November, Bush swept East Texas and crushed Richards' reelection effort. Years later, Rove campaigns used whisper attacks on John McCain in South Carolina, suggesting he had spent too much time in solitary confinement and had a mixed race child out of wedlock.

The Sunday before the election, Bush sat in the backyard of his home in Dallas, lobbing tennis balls into the pool for his dog, Spot, to retrieve. He had been reading Bob Woodward's new book about the workings of the Clinton White House, *The Agenda*. "This guy is mighty fucked up," he told an aide.

His father's loss still gnawed at him, both because he felt Clinton was not worthy of the White House and because his father had failed. Bush took solace in the knowledge that he was going to win; Rove had assured him. He had run his campaign as if it were a war. He had stayed focused and disciplined, never departed from the blueprint.

Bush and Rove, the underestimated candidate and the man with the plan.

They were heading off to make history.

12

Product Launch

The first method for estimating the intelligence of a ruler is to look at the men he has around him.

—Niccolo Machiavelli

Karl Rove never liked George Bush's idea of new business taxes to reduce the property tax burden on homeowners. Texas, Bush had concluded, had spent too many years leaning on the little guy. It was an unusual conclusion for conservative Bush; one he would never make again. Rove always feared that whatever the political benefits of cutting property taxes—and the benefits would be enormous in places like Iowa and New Hampshire—rewriting the state school finance system carried considerable risks.

"The politics of it was butt-ugly," said Rove.

He talked to Bush about the politics of his tax cutting, but the governor decided to move forward anyway.

"His point was, I'm here for big things. He has this sense that leadership matters, that a president or a governor can shape public opinion. So his question is, is this the right thing to do?"

Bush arrived as governor filled with easy confidence. He seemed not so much to walk through the capitol as to glide through it, popping unexpectedly into the offices of legislators, greeting tourists on the steps out front. Bush brought to office an engaging personality and a gift for winning people over, even the mercurial Lt. Governor Bob Bullock. During an early meeting at the Governor's Mansion, Bullock suddenly got angry over some disagreement with the new governor and declared their honeymoon over.

"Okay," Bush said, walking over and throwing his arms around the aging Democrat. "But if you're going to fuck me, I want a kiss first." It was enough to break the ice.

In Bush's first legislative session in 1995, most of his big campaign ideas were enacted into law, largely because the legislature was already considering them.

"He aligned himself with the train that was already moving and got some credit for that," said University of Texas political science professor Bruce Buchanan.

The staff Bush assembled was close-knit and loyal—loyalty was the primary virtue. At the top were Joe Allbaugh, Karen Hughes, and Karl Rove. The three—later dubbed "The Iron Triangle"—were to be the nucleus of Bush's presidential campaign and his White House staff.

Allbaugh, a big-boned Oklahoman with a blond crew cut, replaced Brian Berry as campaign manager following the primary. Berry had grown increasingly irritated over meddling from an influential Bush pal in Dallas and found himself in the middle of a personality spat between the hyperkinetic Rove and press secretary Deborah Burston-Wade.

Hughes, a former TV reporter from Dallas, had made a reputation at the Texas Republican party, where she spent four years softening up Ann Richards with crisp, rapid-response attacks on the Democrat governor's every move. Hughes became a close confidante—smart, direct, exceedingly loyal, and instinctively gifted at managing his image. She was Rove's biggest rival for Bush's ear inside the administration.

In the governor's office, Hughes imposed a strict discipline aimed at controlling the message—a precursor of the White House press office. Calls to the governor's division directors and even some state agency heads were redirected to the press office. Leaks were rare. It was not uncommon for Hughes, whenever the governor found himself straining for a point, to step in and begin fielding the questions herself.

Once, when a reporter began quizzing the governor about campaign contributions at a news conference concerning faith-based organizations, Hughes stepped forward from the side of the room and, her voice booming, took over. All heads turned to Hughes. The governor, long accustomed to this, stopped talking. Hughes simply took command.

Unlike the others, Rove didn't go on the public payroll. He continued to operate his direct-mail business, but he collected a $7,000 monthly retainer from Bush's political account (the real money was in producing campaign material for his stable of political clients) and was an ever-present figure in the Capitol and the Governor's Mansion. Although he was a private consultant, Rove attended virtually every senior staff meeting and had a special phone line installed at his Shoal Creek office exclusively for Bush. He cleared every appointee the governor named, measuring nominations against financial contribution lists, political campaign work, and other tests of Republican orthodoxy.

"Our job is to say is there a significant political problem that would be created by appointing this individual or one by not appointing this individual," he said dryly in a deposition about his informal role as gatekeeper.

A common refrain in the governor's office was: "Where's Karl on this?" or "Has Karl signed off on this?"

Rove wasn't even on the governor's staff, but nothing important happened without his imprimatur. He had achieved a political trifecta, advising appointments to the judiciary, counseling some Republican legislative candidates and serving the chief executive—all three branches of government. He had carried the campaign into the office and turned the office inside out.

Rove became the apotheosis of a "permanent campaign." He ran every discussion of policy through the alembic of politics, evaluating the implications on various groups with a voracious energy, factoring the latest poll results and statistical voter trends. But just as Hughes was sensitive to a precise tone Bush preferred to express an idea, Rove was careful not to present his conclusions as the product of raw politics. That's what Clinton did. Bush was fixated on the idea that Clinton made decisions exclusively on the basis of polls and focus groups. He viewed the administration as so devoid of principle that every action was the product of a shrewd political calculation.

And who better to marshal the armies of substance—demographic data . . . historic models . . . moral constructs . . . legal arguments—to make a policy-based argument than Karl Rove? At senior staff meetings, there was a general understanding that as long as politics wasn't specifically mentioned, politics was not part of the equation, even though everybody knew that Rove had probably already considered the political implications.

Periodically, Bush would swat down his political consultant just to remind everyone who was boss. When the Boston Globe published a story in June 1995 comparing Bush to his father, it quoted Rove: "George W. has a worldview that is significantly different than his father. His father has a sense of noblesse oblige that drives him. George is driven by his desire to make a difference."

Bush was livid. He arrived for a staff meeting and glowered at Rove.

"No one will promote me at the expense of my father. Karl, I expect you to write a handwritten apology."

Rove did write an apology, immediately.

Sometimes, when Rove was particularly puffed up about a particular point, Bush deflated the moment by offering the briefest acknowledgment.

"Thank you, Mr. Big Shot."

Bush was still the boss. But he also knew he would never have gotten the job without Rove. And he also needed Rove for the presidential campaign. They were a team now and neither could succeed without the other.

Tom Pauken was doing nothing for Bush, so far as Rove could see.

Pauken, chairman of the Texas Republican party, had long had a frosty relationship with the Bush family and its allies. He was a Goldwater Republican and former head of the nation's volunteerism agency in the Reagan administration. When he sided with Bob Dole over George Bush in the 1988 presidential race, the younger Bush searched him out at barbecue during the state GOP convention in Houston.

"You son of a bitch, how dare you do this? I'll never forget. You've crossed the line out there," Pauken recalls Bush saying.

Pauken said the message was clear.

"Loyalty is the number one virtue as far as George W. Bush is concerned, but it's loyalty to the Bush family. Everybody is expected to serve the purposes of the Bush family, and if you don't, you have broken the trust and you are no longer in the club."

Karl Rove opposed Pauken's election to head the state Republican party and was outraged two years later when social conservative delegates snubbed Bush, the sitting governor, and made Pauken chairman of the delegation to the GOP national convention in San Diego. Rove convinced the party's blue chip givers to shut off contributions to the state party, effectively rerouting the money to another fund that Rove controlled.

"It was Karl turning the spigot off. He could turn it on, he could turn it off. If you don't play ball, then he's going to make life difficult."

As Bush prepared to introduce his school tax plan to the 1997 legislative session, he feared Pauken would be a problem. His plan to cut property taxes by $3 billion would require raising the sales tax and creating a new business tax—both anathemas to staunch conservatives like Pauken. Even if the average Texan ended up paying less in taxes overall, he knew Pauken wouldn't like it. Bush summoned the party chief to the capitol.

"You have to support this," Bush said.

"I don't know enough about it, but I have some concerns."

"No. You've got to support this."

Pauken was resolute.

"Can't do it. It's not personal, governor. It's just something I'm philosophically opposed to."

The Bush plan was in trouble from the beginning. The right didn't like the tax hikes. The left was suspicious big beneficiaries were likely to be companies like Enron and the petrochemical giants. Representative Paul Sadler, a brilliant East Texas trial lawyer who was to become Bush's most important ally in the House, wondered as he listened to the governor deliver his speech in the immense House chamber what had happened to his friend, George Bush, whose passion two years earlier seemed to be education, not tax cuts.

"Somewhere between '95 and '97 he got off message and it bothered me," said Sadler. "He was talking about how we've got to do something about property taxes, property taxes, property taxes. He wanted to separate property taxes from school finance, which is an impossible thing to do in Texas. He got strictly on property tax relief and I couldn't figure out why."

By 1997, as Bush's name began popping up among future presidential candidates, tax cuts had become the end. Bush appointed a committee to conduct statewide hearings, dubbed "the tax road show." Rossanna Salazar, a respected former aide to Governor Bill Clements, was tapped at Rove's behest to help promote the committee and generated bundles of fresh press clippings, which a staff assembled amid the thrum of photocopiers in the basement of the Capitol.

"I'd go down there to get the clips and Rove would always be down there. It was like he had an office down there in the basement," said Cindy Rugeley, who worked on the promotion effort.

Former Governor Bill Clements called, concerned that the politics of shifting business taxes would undo Bush's future. Sipple, the campaign's ad man, sent a note warning that the downside risks seemed to outweigh any upside advantages. But Bush had now staked too much on the idea and moved forward.

Before the legislature convened, Bush held a news conference next to the gazebo on the grounds of the Governor's Mansion and publicly laid claim to $1 billion of surplus in the state budget to cut taxes. "I started getting worried," said Sadler. "You've got a Republican governor who's talking about property tax relief, not school finance, which is what the issue should be."

Sadler shelved the Bush proposal and his House committee began working on a plan of its own. What surprised Sadler was how quickly Bush came around to the committee's view. He and Bush struck up a strong friendship. And as they talked—long, deep conversations about education and taxes, about family and the future—it was clear to Sadler that Bush was very much committed to improving public education in Texas. He was remarkably open to other ideas for financing schools and altering the tax system—ideas he apparently never considered or were never presented.

As they met in Bush's office at the capitol or talked into the evening over coffee and cigars at the mansion, Sadler grew to understand in a vivid way exactly how Bush thinks and makes decisions.

Bush's gift, Sadler came to believe, was his ability to sift through the various recommendations and come to a crisp, final decision.

"I have absolutely no question in his ability to make the right decision if he's presented the facts from all sides. I have watched him do it. Where I found he gets off track is if he only has once voice in the room. There's what's always bothered me," said Sadler.

For months, the Sadler committee worked on its version of the school tax bill, inviting hundreds of people to testify with ideas. Lawmakers poured through the Byzantine filigree of school finance, its formulas, and its assumptions. The result was a plan that gave property tax relief to homeowners and boosted state spending on schools. The bill was guaranteed to attract opposition from some business groups—it shifted some taxes around—but Bush adopted it as his own. This was the premier issue of his governorship, and he laid his credibility on the line by urging passage by the Senate.

Bush worked the bill, lobbied, and cajoled. On the Saturday it all fell apart, Bush was exhausted from long hours, frayed tempers.

"We had been to hell and back," said Sadler.

But in the end, the coterie of Republican senators refused to go along. Florence Shapiro said no and now the room was nearly empty and Bush slumped in the chair.

He turned to the two Democratic legislators, Mark Stiles and Paul Sadler.

"What do you think I should do?" he asked.

"What do you want to do? Who are you trying to help, governor?" Stiles asked.

Bush paused.

"I want to help the poorest Texas homeowner."

There would be no massive property tax relief, no long-term fix for the state's school finance problems. But there was still $1 billion in surplus available for a modest tax cut for homeowners.

"Take the billion dollars," Sadler said.

Bush put his head in his hands and his eyes welled up with tears.

"I did not know how to read his emotion," said Sadler. "I didn't know if it was disappointment that something good was going down. I didn't know if it was, 'My political future is over.' I didn't know what it meant and I didn't want to ask. I really didn't want to know."

The next day, Sadler got word that Bush wanted to see him in his office. This time, his staff surrounded Bush, including education chief Margaret LaMontagne and press secretary Karen Hughes. Bush said they had decided to apply the $1 billion outside the school-finance formula. This meant teachers wouldn't get a pay raise.

"They've never been with us," Hughes said of the teacher unions.

This did not sound like Hughes. It didn't sound like Bush or La-Montagne. This had a hard, political edge. This sounded like Rove.

Sadler protested and after some argument, Bush relented and teachers got a raise. Once Bush was presented with a wider range of voices in the room, once he went outside his small circle of advisors, he made a better judgment. But the sour impression of that moment stayed with Sadler into the next legislative session in 1999, when Bush rolled out his last legislative agenda as governor.

It was an agenda befitting a presidential campaign.

This time, there were no complex school-tax proposals that might alienate business. Instead, there was a strong ideological bent guaranteed to find favor among Republican primary voters. Bush advocated stricter limits on abortion. He pledged to end the practice of automatically passing students, a theme consistent with the conservative message of personal responsibility. His legislative lobby team kept a hate-crimes bill bottled up and away from his desk. School vouchers, something Bush hadn't pushed in years, were back on his agenda. As a new governor, Bush had privately assured Sadler, "Don't worry about vouchers." But now school vouchers were suddenly important again.

"Where did this voucher stuff come from?" Sadler asked. "He just grinned at me."

Most important, tax cuts were back, this time a neat $2 billion in tax relief from budget surplus—and the governor fought every effort to whittle down the amount. When lawmakers tried to put money into a pre-kindergarten program, Bush resisted. When the legislature needed money to fund a teacher health program, Bush fought it.

"What's so magic about the number $2 billion?" Sadler asked. "Why isn't $1.9 billion enough? Why isn't $1.8 billion enough?"

"I just have to have $2 billion," Bush said.

"You want $2 billion because you have to beat Christie [Gov. of New Jersey] Todd Whitman," Sadler said.

Bush's agenda was Rove's agenda.

"When I'm asked about his management style, I say look to the dominant personality. Look to the person he trusts the most, and that's the person he'll ultimately go to," said Sadler.

"I will tell you, I have been concerned many times since September 11 because of that. Because I know how he makes decisions. I know how he does it. And I've watched as they have drawn that circle up there, closer and closer and tighter. And I know who's in the middle of it, and it bothers me a lot."

When the plane touched down in Cedar Rapids, Iowa, under a crystal-bright sky in June 1999, the crowd corralled in a huge metal airplane hanger began waving signs and cheering for the governor of Texas, who was making his first campaign stop of the 2000 presidential race.

The 727 arrived bursting with a full Bush entourage and the squeaking, beeping mob of the national news media, which streamed down the stairway to capture every sight and sound. There was NBC. There was CNN. There, at the top of the stairway, were Bush and his wife, Laura, waving to the jubilant crowd.

"I'm ready," Bush declared. "There's no turning back. I intend to be president of the United States."

The crowd and the cameras all followed Bush, the candidate. Rove blinked as he stepped out into the bright Iowa sun and descended the stairway of the plane dubbed Great Expectations. They were now in Iowa, the first test of the 2000 presidential race, the land of cornfields and political caucuses. A candidate had arrived with the credentials to be president of the United States—a compassionate conservative, an advocate of personal responsibility and a champion of tax cuts with the nice, round $2 billion to show for it.

Brian Berry, who Rove had fired for questioning his tactics, was watching television and marveled at how Bush and Rove had made it, how they were finally in Iowa.

"They were long friends and this was a long dream."

13

Everything Matters

An expert is a man who has made all the mistakes which can be
made in a very narrow field.

—Niels Bohr

As it turned out, Rove was wrong about New Hampshire.
He was depending on intelligence from Senator Judd
Gregg's organization and from his own political contacts.
Mostly, he was depending on poll numbers, his Cartesian
tellers of truth, which never failed him, not if properly analyzed.
And nobody could analyze the numbers like Karl Rove.

"Look here!" he said, hunched over a small square table at the
Days Inn in Merrimack.

On the table was a napkin with a series of lines drawn like jagged
horizons, rising and falling, sometimes crossing. The lines represented different poll results. There were recent network polls and
Republican Party polls and the Bush campaign's own polling. One of
the lines represented something called PortraitofAmerica.com, a
Web site that Rove pored over daily in his voracious search for every
tic and shift in American opinion.

"Look at the trends. We're going to win New Hampshire," Rove declared. He pointed to the napkin and explained that the momentum, which initially seemed to favor Bush and then McCain, now favored Bush again. Bush's numbers were on the ascendancy and, given time, he would overcome McCain. By Rove's calculation, there was time before the February 1 New Hampshire primary, the first in the nation. So now he was bouncing around in the plastic chair in the snack bar of the motel, confident, exultant.

Outside, the snow had stopped falling. Inside, in the bright reflected light, Rove was in full-turbo mode, offering up a lavishly dense explanation about cross-tabs and voter trends and New England historical precedents as evidence of an impending Bush victory.

Why not? The ghosts were all good for George W. Bush in New Hampshire, starting in June 1999. Two weeks after the legislative session ended, Bush launched his maiden campaign trip, first to Iowa and then on to New Castle, New Hampshire, where a news conference was arranged under a white tent against a backdrop of New England coastline.

Every national newspaper, magazine, and network had sent reporters. Maureen Dowd of the *New York Times* sat on the front row, wearing sunglasses. Chris Matthews of MSNBC stood among the cluster of camera crews. Thick fog had settled over the coast, obscuring the lighthouse that was to have provided a picturesque backdrop.

"This was his debut on the national stage, the big moment. And you could smell fear in the air," said Mark McKinnon, Bush's television media consultant. "You could sense the press just ready to put him through his paces and see if he was ready. He was up there on the high wire for the first time without a net and some of us in the campaign were very nervous and I think he was, too."

Rove and Hughes and McKinnon all knew this was a moment of no small import. "It was a new jungle and new animals," said McKinnon.

The team watched their man step onto the platform. Bush assumed a veneer of confidence, but his body language telegraphed apprehension. He offered stiff answers to the first volley of questions.

"It was almost like one of those Arnold Schwarzenegger movies where all the dials in his brain were surveying the room and downloading information. Danger! Danger! Heat-seeking here! Friendly fire over there!" said McKinnon.

Then, about five minutes into the news conference, Bush's shoulders started to relax and his arms fell easily at his side. He rolled slightly on his hips, like a quarterback throwing an easy spiral.

"Matthews," Bush said, singling him out in the crowd. "It's good to see the larger personalities are starting to show up."

The fear in the Bush camp began to dissipate.

"I remember literally seeing the moment when he physically changed and was saying, 'I can do this,'" McKinnon said.

In the months that followed, Bush sought to cultivate the national press in much the way he had done in Austin—with attention and flattery and a talent for suggesting they were seeing in his informality a glimpse of the inner man. This was not so much Rove's doing as Hughes'. She recognized the value of Bush's engaging personality and arranged that he wander up and down the center aisle, making small talk with every reporter. Although Bush privately was wary of reporters, he had confidence in his ability to make friends and influence antagonists.

But there were disconcerting signs in New Hampshire, which Rove and the rest of the Austin crew did not take seriously enough. Bush skipped two early debates in New Hampshire, which rankled some supporters. When Hughes visited the state in late 1999, she went to Bush campaign headquarters and noticed that almost all the volunteers were from somewhere else.

"I thought, that doesn't seem right," Hughes said, but then disregarded it like so many other signals that the Bush effort wasn't going well.

Rove did not see the McCain challenge until it was too late. He was immersed in the master plan—Bush campaign organizations in all 50 states, the hierarchy of the Republican Party falling in line: Certain victory by March.

"If you are the establishment choice on the Republican side, you are the inevitable nominee. No ifs, ands, or buts," Rove told a group of Austin business lobbyists at a private luncheon 10 weeks before the New Hampshire primary.

"At the end of the day, there will be 30 members of the 55 Republicans in the U.S. Senate for George W. Bush, despite the fact that one of their own is running. More important, a majority of Republicans in 32 state legislatures have endorsed George W. Bush."

The Republican leadership had, indeed, fallen in with Bush, seduced by his front-runner status and a carefully orchestrated succession of visits to Austin conceived by Rove in the manner of William McKinley's "front-porch campaign" a century earlier. Mark Hanna was the key architect in 1896, bringing a procession of prominent visitors to McKinley's modest home in Canton and effectively locking up the Republican nomination. Now it was Rove engineering the flow of Republicans to Austin in early 1999. Governors and state legislators came.

"We're going to face a series of sequential battles," Rove said. "In Iowa, there'll be Forbes. In New Hampshire, it's going to be McCain."

He suggested New Hampshire was well in hand, although he was oddly critical of the voters there.

"They're crazy. They like being obstreperous and they want you to spend a lot of time there. As of the 18th of October, McCain had spent more on media in New Hampshire than we did. He had used one-third of the money he can spend. There will not be a single day from here to the end of the campaign where he will outspend us on TV and message."

Still, Rove remained confident of his national strategy to compete everywhere, and ride as the front-runner above the rabble. Bush's first appearance on a Sunday morning show was with Tim Russert on NBC's *Meet the Press*. Russert had been aggressive about courting Bush, flying to Austin months earlier to meet informally with the governor, staying at a hotel near the Governor's Mansion, stopping by the Texas Chili Parlor to soak up some Austin atmosphere with the regulars. Bush could introduce himself to a national audience and, Rove was confident, help dispel the idea that he was dumb. As a measure of preparation for the show, Rove presented Bush a list of every question Russert had ever asked about Bush on *Meet the Press*. Bush, true to form, gave the list scant attention.

"He looked over it briefly," said Hughes.

Bush did well on the show, in part because Rove and Hughes had worked to lower expectations, but also because Bush appeared to have a grasp of the issues.

By the time he arrived in New Hampshire, fresh off his win in the Iowa caucuses, Bush was trailing the runaway McCain campaign in the polls. Forbes was a distant third. But Rove took heart in tracking polls that showed Bush gaining and he assured the governor victory was possible.

In fact, Bush was doomed.

McCain had struck a deep and receptive nerve in the cranky voters of New Hampshire, a yearning for a hero, a maverick, a leader who would crash the party of politics as usual. Bush talked about restoring the dignity of the office, but McCain seemed to embody the idea. Bush arrived in a private jet with his entourage following in the 737. McCain had been on the ground for weeks, preaching the message of reform in the back of a bus called the Straight Talk Express that bumped along the snowy highways from Milford to Portsmouth to Merrimack.

Rove held firm to the idea that the strategy—stay positive, stay presidential—could work. He saw it in the numbers on the napkin as he sat in the snack bar area of the motel in Merrimack. He saw in the tangle of polling numbers the potential for Bush to overtake McCain in the final days of the primary and to emerge with what he called "a nomination that is worth having." In the final days, Bush went snowmobiling. And sledding. And candlepin bowling.

While Bush toured the Department of Safety headquarters in Concord with a press pool, Rove and reporters in the parking lot began lobbing snowballs at each other. Rove quickly escalated the pace.

He stood in the lot lined with mounds of snow and threw snowballs with a manic energy. He threw and threw, bashing a reporter in the head a few yards away, taking a splattering shot to the back of his overcoat. He scooped up snow and threw with such force that he seemed like a machine, throwing again and again, sweating in the bright chill of the day, flailing wildly against his enemies, beyond fatigue, beyond any reasonable limit of play.

This was no casual snowball fight, but a war. He didn't simply want to win; he wanted to crush his opponents. He wanted his enemies to flee. Standing in the snow-covered parking lot, battered and triumphant, Rove began jeering at the opposition. He strutted back and forth along a line, offering himself like a target in a shooting gallery. Snowballs came in on a long arc, but he dodged them.

"Missed me!" he taunted.

His face was ruddy with exhilaration and fatigue, his hair matted against his head. Many in the press had retreated to the bus.

"Losers!" Rove yelled, the darkest insult he could dredge up, the most denigrating label he could imagine.

"LOSERS!"

The night Bush lost New Hampshire, Rove made the telephone call to McCain's hotel suite. An aide answered, but the voice in the background belonged to John Weaver, McCain's political director.

"Consultants don't concede to candidates," Weaver instructed the aide to say.

This was McCain's night, and the protocols of such a night required that the losing candidate make the concession call and wait on the line for the winner, not the other way around. As it turned out, the Bush campaign didn't have a phone number for McCain, so Rove asked Alexandra Pelosi, an NBC producer who was shooting footage for her documentary, *Journeys with George*. Pelosi did have the number on her cell phone and did give it to Rove, but in exchange she wanted to film Bush making his concession speech. Rove agreed and took the phone, but later reneged on his deal with Pelosi. There would be no pictures of Bush conceding defeat.

When a McCain aide answered, Rove asked if this were the right number for Bush to call. But Weaver was insulted that Rove . . . his arch-enemy Karl Rove . . . was calling with any expectation that McCain would come to the phone. Weaver's message was clear: You lost, we won, tell Bush to make the call.

Bush did make the call. It lasted 90 seconds.

"John, you ran a great race, congratulations."

"Thanks for calling," said McCain. "We've run a campaign that you and I and our families can be proud of."

Weaver was exuberant with the results in New Hampshire, not that you could tell by looking at him. He was a tall, thin ex-Texan who wore on his face a perpetual look of worry. McCain nicknamed him "Sunny" as a joke because he clearly was not. He was dour, forever suspicious of the tactics of political opponents, and he carried in his head brilliant political instincts that associates back in Texas said made him every bit the equal of Rove.

They had been good friends 15 years earlier, had planned to go into business together—the two best young political minds in Texas in one shop. When Bill Clements won the Republican nomination for governor in 1986, Rove got Weaver the job as deputy campaign manager. They worked well together, Rove the outside consultant and Weaver the inside manager. Clements won and was so impressed he asked Weaver what he wanted. What Weaver wanted was to be executive director of the Texas Republican party.

It was then that the friction started between Rove and Weaver, according to political associates. In the 1988 presidential race, Weaver met with George Herbert Walker Bush in a hotel suite in Houston and, with Clements' backing, the future president hand-picked him to head the Bush campaign in Texas, Victory '88.

The Republican party had a finite budget for the 1988 race and established a plan allocating sums for television and radio commercials, direct-mail advertising, salaries, phone banks, the light bill—everything required to operate a successful campaign. Rove's firm had the direct-mail account.

"Karl was really permissive in the way he did the mail. And he started doing some mail that didn't necessarily get approved or disapproved. When he was doing mail early on, he was trying to generate revenue, so Karl was pushing mail," said a Republican colleague.

Weaver, sitting at party headquarters, saw Rove's invoices roll in for work never formally approved. Weaver decided to pull rank and warned Rove that no work should be done without his okay. When he felt the order had been violated, Weaver refused to pay.

"He made Karl eat the cost. It was a lot of money," said the Republican.

"Weaver and Karl were very much alike—two bulls in a china shop."

Weaver decided to start his own consulting firm and hired Rove's ace copywriter, John Colyandro. Stole him, the way Rove saw it.

Colyandro called it a personal decision, something he wanted to do to develop professionally. "But Karl was not pleased with that," he said. "My team, your team—that's the way he's always conducted himself."

The acrimony between Rove and Weaver grew. Rove lost some national clients and blamed Weaver. When Rob Mosbacher Jr., the son of President Bush's commerce secretary, took over the 1992 Bush reelection committee in Texas, he gave Weaver the big direct-mail account. Rove had a small contract for fund-raising, but Weaver had the important business of mass-mailing campaign appeals directly to voters. In September, a syndicated column by Roland Evans and Robert Novak appeared in newspapers suggesting the Texas reelection committee was in disarray and that President Bush was in danger of losing his home state.

The column said a secret meeting of worried Republican power brokers was held in Dallas in mid-September and that Mosbacher had been stripped of his authority and replaced by a Rove ally, Jim Francis. The column said Mosbacher "has been attacked for running the Victory '92 Committee out of Houston as a personal 1994 launching pad for governor." Several Republicans active in party affairs at the time said there was, indeed, criticism of Mosbacher's handling of the committee—from Rove.

After the column appeared, Phil Gramm issued a news release defending Mosbacher and making it clear he remained very much at the helm of Victory '92. Rove's contract was terminated. But the damage had been done to Mosbacher and, by extension, to Weaver. Rove had his own candidate in mind for governor in 1994 and it wasn't going to be Team Mosbacher.

"The thing that separates Karl from other people is his determination," said Colyandro. "Despite setbacks, whether on a business level or a personal level, he remains dogged. Look at the bodies on the political battlefield and they refused to remain dogged and determined. That determination, that's what separates Karl from the rest of the crowd."

What was obvious, though, was that Rove had leaked information, his perception of things, to the columnists. And that the Bush campaign believed Rove had given the negative impressions to Robert Novak because no reporter in Texas was willing to write the story. Rove was subsequently fired and, during the run-up to the Iraq War, the incident increased speculation that Rove had been the person to leak the name of an undercover CIA agent as an act of vengeance against her husband, a former ambassador who was a Bush critic.

In everything Rove did, he played to win. He simply worked harder and longer and with an intensity that burned the edges of the field of play. His second wife, Darby, told a reporter for the *New York Times* that Karl had learned to "lay back a little bit" when playing chess with their young son, Andrew. "But even in croquet he'd be hitting my ball so far I was crying on vacation."

"I told Karl the other day," she said, "You see things in black and white. I see lots of gray."

No one was immune to his manic energy and competitive zeal. No candidate, no operative, no journalist.

Even Rove's neighbor, a dentist named Joe Neely, came to understand that. Neely was a fit and youthful-looking baby boomer with a good practice in Austin. He and his wife built a house among the hills and cedar breaks just west of Austin, along the pitch and turn of the Balcones Fault. It was a beautiful neighborhood, festooned with trees and divided into lots from two to seven acres, which assured some distance between the homes. Rove bought the lot next door, physically moved a century-old farmhouse onto the property and, with his wife, Darby, set about restoring it.

"One day, I'm coming home and right in front of our front door, in front of our house, there are a bunch of concrete forms up. I thought what the heck is that?" said Neely. "I mean dead on the property line as close to our property as you can get, set slightly before and looking into our master bath."

Neely knocked on his neighbor's door and Rove told him he was building a garage. Neely wasn't happy about it, but Rove assured him that he would plant trees to block the view. A construction crew laid the foundation, and then framed the first story. But when builders began erecting a second story, an apparent violation of deed restrictions, Neely had his lawyer call Rove to complain.

Rove directed that everybody meet at his house—Rove, Neely, the lawyers. He opened with an appeal to continue building the garage, but when it became clear that Neely wasn't going to budge, Rove's face grew dark.

"He started yelling and screaming and demanding I get off his property and never speak to him again. I'm just dumbfounded."

Eventually, after the lawyers talked, Rove dismantled the structure down to the slab. Neely planted some trees on his property to block the view of the concrete and figured the matter was ended.

One day, several months later, Neely got a call. One of the trees had died and there was a message on his answering machine. . . . "Tear down that tree. . . ."

Neely did and heard nothing more. Karl, Darby, and son Andrew had been long-time dental patients, but no longer. From then on, the neighbors did not talk, not for years—and only spoke again after Neely veered too close to the property line one day trimming a cluster of bluebonnets that had gone to seed. Rove called to complain, saying Neely had encroached on his land by 30 to 40 feet. He ordered Neely to meet him at the property line.

"My kids are loving this. They think it's high noon. So I got out there and he will not walk across onto my property and has taken a bunch of little survey flags and has stuck the flags into the ground right in front of our house." Neely apologized and promised it wouldn't happen again.

"I'm sorry about what happened five years ago with your garage," Neely told Rove. "And I'm sorry about your bluebonnets. But I've had it with you calling and leaving pugnacious, vitriolic messages on my answering machine."

Then Neely remembered his neighbor saying something remarkable, something so unexpected he didn't know how to respond.

"You just don't get it," said Rove.

"Get what?"

"What you said to me five years ago."

Neely did not know what he was talking about.

"You said you moved out here to get away from people like me."

Neely was flabbergasted. He could not imagine ever having said that. He was surprised how Rove had internalized this squabble between neighbors and made it so thoroughly personal. Beneath all the bravura, Rove seemed deeply unsure of himself. People . . . like me. What could he mean? That he was not some yuppie Austin professional? That he lacked the ease and social skills of his modestly prosperous neighbors? Neely denied ever saying anything like that.

"Now you're calling me a liar, huh?"

Neely almost laughed. This was not about settling an argument. This was about winning, Rove winning. He seemed to be driven by a roaring internal engine to control every disagreement, rule every dispute, and dominate every contest. In everything he did, Karl Rove wanted to win.

When it turned out he was wrong about New Hampshire and Bush lost, it was something Rove seemed to take personally.

The early exit polls gave some measure of the size of the defeat. Shortly after noon, Rove went across the hall at the Residence Inn in Merrimack and gave Bush the bad news that the early numbers had McCain up by 19 points.

"What the hell happened?" Bush asked.

Rove didn't have an answer, not a good one. He was surprised by the huge number of independents who came into the primary, an unprecedented outpouring of people drawn by McCain's reformist themes. Rove reasserted confidence in his 50-state strategy. McCain could not keep up, he said. "He's done. He's got the positive side of it. Now we'll see if there's much more positive side. I don't think there is."

The strategy for beating McCain in South Carolina came in two parts. First, Bush needed to invert the formula that McCain was the reformer and Bush the politician. Hughes proposed a new slogan for Bush—Reformer With Results—and a new emphasis on the idea that McCain was the true Washington insider. The other part of the Bush strategy was darker and had a more mysterious genesis. It resembled the sour mash tactics of the Lee Atwater days, a hard, negative assault on the opponent, sometimes directly and sometimes under cover. It was the approach favored by Rove. . . . Attack, Attack, Attack . . . only now, apparently, Bush was very much on the program.

A new Bush television commercial branded McCain a hypocrite, a champion of reform who filled his treasury with thousands of dollars in contributions from corporate political action committees. Meanwhile, Bush inadvertently previewed another part of campaign strategy during a rally in a conversation picked up by a C-Span microphone.

"Y'all haven't even hit his soft spots," said state Senator Mike Fair, a Bush supporter.

"We're going to," Bush replied, but added he was "not going to do it on TV."

What followed were two weeks of slaughterhouse politics in Dixie.

The Bush camp launched saturation TV and radio attacks. It sent direct-mail warnings that McCain wanted to remove the pro-life plank from the GOP, which wasn't true but stirred the attention of the state's sizable population of antiabortion voters. Rove had recruited Ralph Reed, formerly of the Christian Coalition, to help bring out religious conservatives. Surrogates accused the Arizona senator, a former prisoner of war, of abandoning his Vietnam veterans. A professor from Bob Jones sent out an e-mail claiming McCain had fathered illegitimate children. Bush's polling firm made several hundred so-called "push-poll" telephone calls asking harsh questions about McCain. And other calls, which the Bush campaign declared were not its doing, presented even darker warnings: Cindy McCain had drug problems and the McCains had a black child.

The succession of attacks—some clearly from the Bush camp, some from supporters likely acting alone in the superheated political stew of South Carolina—angered McCain, who believed them a betrayal of the high campaign standards that Bush had so publicly proclaimed. Before the South Carolina debate, as the two men stood awkwardly next to each other in the studio, McCain turned on his rival.

"George," he said, slowing shaking his head.

"John," Bush replied, then added as if by explanation, "It's politics."

"George, everything isn't politics."

During a commercial break, McCain complained that Bush supporters had leveled a savage direct-mail and phone campaign against him. Bush expressed innocence. He reached over to grasp his rival's hand and said the two should put their acrimony behind them.

"Don't give me that shit," said McCain, pulling away. "And take your hands off me."

Bush beat McCain by 11 points in South Carolina. Rove was expansive in victory.

"People in this state wanted to know that he was willing to fight for it. Was he a guy who had the ability to pick himself up off the mat, dust himself off, wipe off the blood, and go back in there."

Rove was the architect of Bush's sharp turn to the right. But the move carried consequences, most notably the primary three days later in Michigan, where McCain forces were already trumpeting Bush's embrace of Bob Jones University, which not only had restrictions about interracial dating but also a distinct anti-Catholic bias. A big bloc of voters in Michigan were Catholic and Rove watched as Weaver and the rest of the McCainiacs launched their own counteroffensive, effectively dubbing Bush an anti-Catholic bigot.

Bush lost, but Michigan was McCain's last stand. The general election, Bush and Rove knew, would require the candidate to move back toward the middle. The first step was to shore up Catholic support with a letter to Cardinal John O'Connor apologizing for the Bob Jones visit, which Bush solemnly read before a battery of TV cameras.

"On reflection, I should have been more clear in disassociating myself from anti-Catholic sentiment and racial prejudice. It was a missed opportunity causing needless offense, which I deeply regret."

Still, Bush was miffed by the McCain insurgency in Michigan. He said as much, chatting casually with a couple of reporters on his plane.

"I couldn't believe anybody who would think I'm an anti-Catholic bigot," Bush said.

The reporters questioned whether the letter to the cardinal was sufficient. In a startling gesture, Bush pulled out a penknife, opened the blade, and put it to his throat.

"What do you want? I just ate crow on national TV?"

"Jim Crow, I believe," one reporter fired back, and everyone laughed, Bush most of all.

Bush was two days from his win in the Washington primary, and about a week from Super Tuesday, the mother of all primaries, which was to seal his nomination. George W. Bush, sailing aloft at 40,000 feet, was a very happy man. He was about to become the Republican nominee for president.

And Karl Rove, back in Austin, was already thinking ahead to the fall campaign.

14

Whose Dream Is This, Anyway?

> We thought, because we had power, we had wisdom.
> —Stephen Vincent Benet

It was 5 A.M. and George W. Bush couldn't sleep. He had been on the road more than a year in pursuit of the presidency, traveling from city to city, waking up in the indistinguishable dark of yet another hotel room. Bush got up, put on some running clothes and poked his head out the door.

"Can't sleep," he said. "I want to work out now."

The security contingent, stationed overnight outside his door, followed the candidate outside for a brisk, three-mile morning run. A faint red sunrise streaked the sky and nothing was moving, just Bush, running through the streets of yet another city, turning now along a river where the moon rode as its reflection on the water.

Returning to the motel, Bush asked a member of his security detail about his travel aide, Logan Walters.

"Have you seen Logan?"

Walters, the diminutive, exceedingly attentive aide, was sleeping in the room directly across the hall. The schedule wasn't set to start until 10:30 A.M.

"Do you want me to wake him up?" asked a member of his security.

"No," Bush said and went into his room.

He emerged two minutes later, walked directly to Logan's room and began loudly knocking. The sleepy-eyed travel aide fumbled to open the door, then stood blinking in the doorway.

"Logan, are we at war?" Bush said.

Logan struggled to comprehend the question, and then his eyes grew wide.

"What? We're at war?"

"Logan, this is war. We've been at war for 12 months. And when I'm ready to go, you've got to be ready to go."

Bush then turned, and with the wry grin of a fraternity prankster winked at his security detail, disappeared into his room and went back to bed. A few minutes later, Logan stepped out into the hallway, freshly bathed, and fully dressed, packed and ready to go. He waited, patiently, for three hours for the events of the day to begin.

This became a refrain between Bush and his aide—"Logan, are we at war?"—more banter than call to preparation. In the wake of 9/11, the exchange has an odd, discordant feel. Bush the future commander in chief at war, pretending to be the commander in chief at war.

At the time, in the heart of a political campaign, the remark was more about camaraderie than statecraft. It was Bush the DEKE, having fun on the trail while Rove the drudge, back at headquarters in Austin, worked the phones.

And Rove was always on the phone.

The Bush for President Headquarters was a vast warren of cubicles and office spaces on the second floor of a red granite bank building in downtown Austin. There was a guard desk and a full security force protecting against anyone who lacked the proper credentials and electronic access cards. Rove had a small office cluttered with boxes and files where he walked around with the receiver to his ear, gesticulating wildly, pealing orders with the brisk authority of a general.

Stashed in one of the boxes was a framed picture of himself—rail-thin and wearing a Madras sports coat—with Bill Clements, his first big candidate in Texas. On the wall above the paper shredder was his portrait of Theodore Roosevelt, patron saint of vigorous, hard-charging Republicanism.

Even as the campaign fell into what McKinnon called "Black September," the post-convention period in which Gore rose in the polls and the attacks on Bush seemed to be working, Rove wore a confident look. He bought ice cream every week for the campaign staff. He presided over meetings with a cheery optimism. In the Gore attack designed to portray Bush as dense and dangerously ill-prepared, Rove saw a history lesson. Ronald Reagan vs. Jimmy Carter, the insurgent and the status quo.

"In 1980, it's a relatively close race. The party in power was not able to take advantage. People are inclined toward the challenger," Rove said one day at campaign headquarters. "There's a ceiling to what Carter is going to get. The question in the end is whether people need to be reassured that Reagan is acceptable."

The key, then and now, was reassurance. Voters, not just the party's conservative base but Midwestern soccer moms and moderate suburbanites, had to feel comfortable with Bush. The first step was visual, large crowds and bursts of confetti, a Latino rally in Philadelphia to open Bush's arrival for the Republican National Convention, a speech in which his largest national audience might see him as presidential.

"It's all visuals," Rove told campaign finance chief Don Evans. "You campaign as if America was watching TV with the sound turned down. It's all visuals."

By late summer, Professor James Thurber of American University, an expert in presidential politics, saw in the Bush campaign some evidence that its emphasis on personality and its appeal to a wider audience was working.

"George W. has very simple messages, but they're remembered to a certain extent by those who are watching the campaign," Thurber said in an interview. "He might not be the brightest guy around, but we've had a lot of presidents who weren't. He's not scaring people as much as he was at the beginning."

After tacking so far to the right in the primaries, Bush needed to steer a course back to the center—or at least appear to do so. He obviously understood the campaign had to send signals that would keep the conservative base in the line and still expand Bush's appeal among moderates. The conservatives would sign off on Bush's policies; the moderates needed reassurance about his record. "Political heuristics," Rove called it.

When Bush took the stage in 2000, he spoke forcefully about the need to protect the border with Mexico, but compassionately about the reality that immigrants will continue to enter so long as they can earn $5 an hour in America instead of 50 cents in Mexico. It was a message to two separate groups. Conservatives heard the part about protecting the border and the superiority of America. Moderates saw a Republican who recognized immigrants as people. The sentiment was Bush, but the political packaging was pure Rove.

Through three sessions of the Texas Legislature, Rove advised Bush with an eye on cultivating his conservative base without alienating voters in the middle. The Bush record was about large tax cuts, stronger student testing, greater local control for school districts. He preached personal responsibility. He never had to deal with a hate-crimes bill opposed by Christian conservatives, thanks to Republicans who bottled up the measure in committee.

Rove even tried to manage the results of the 1998 reelection race in Texas to enhance Bush's appeal in 2000, even if it meant sacrificing fellow Republicans in the process.

In 1998, Bush was assured of reelection. His popularity ratings were high, his Democratic opponent was weak and Rove was tapping an ever-larger national network of financial contributors. While Bush was far ahead in the polls, Republican ticket mate Rick Perry was locked in a very close race. Worried they were about to lose, the Perry team produced a television commercial late in the campaign attacking his Democratic opponent.

Rove, who was not even Perry's consultant, ordered the commercial killed.

"You're not going to run this spot," Rove instructed. "And if you run this spot, we're going to pull the Bush 41 endorsement spot that you'd planned to run at the end."

According to a Perry campaign aide, Rove's primary goal was to drive the numbers for Bush as high as possible, not only among White voters but also among Hispanics and African Americans who typically vote Democrat. To do that, Rove decided he only wanted positive commercials by Republican candidates on TV in the campaign's closing weeks.

"Their thinking was we want to get 68 percent of the vote instead of 67 percent or 66 percent of the vote," the Perry aide said. "We don't want to fuck up the political environment. It's the ultimate calculation on Karl's part that says Perry doesn't need to do that, that he can still win."

The Perry team feared Perry could not win, not without airing the attack spot against his Democratic opponent. But they also needed to close with the televised endorsement of former President George Bush, and Rove controlled the Bush commercial.

Perry, fearing he was about to be sacrificed, had no choice but to follow Rove's orders.

On Election Day, Bush won with 68 percent of the vote, swamping his opponent by 1.4 million votes—a testament to Bush's broad appeal that Rove trumpeted in the presidential race.

Perry also won, barely, by 68,731 votes.

"It was either calculated genius or arrogance," said the Perry aide.

Either way, it turned out Rove was right.

I've won," said George W. Bush, one week before Election Day. A couple of reporters on the plane appeared unconvinced. But Bush was supremely confident, leaning against the bulkhead with a Buckler near-beer in his hand.

"I have access to more information."

As it turned out, the Bush campaign righted itself in October after the September slide. Karen Hughes had produced a new slogan—Real Plans for Real People—which had the twin benefit of suggesting there was something unreal not only about Gore's ideas, but about Gore himself. More importantly, Bush exceeded expectations in three televised debates.

"People wanted to know if he could share the stage with Gore," said media chief Mark McKinnon.

Now the campaign rolled into its final days, pursuing what the Bush team called the DFIU strategy—don't fuck it up. Then the DUI story hit.

In September 1976, at age 30, Bush was arrested for drunken driving while in Kennebunkport visiting his parents. News of the two-decade-old arrest broke first on a television station in Maine, and then Fox News went with the story. Bush pleaded guilty in the case, paid a $150 fine and had his driving privileges suspended in Maine. Throughout his campaigns for governor and for president, Bush had sought to keep the episode secret, saying only that he had made unspecified mistakes in his youth.

Word of the arrest shot through the Bush press corps. Hughes, realizing her boss needed to confront the issue, gathered reporters outside the brick cattle barn at State Fair Park in West Allys, Wisconsin, for a late-night news conference.

"I'm the first to say what I did is wrong and I corrected that," Bush said, blinking into a blazing bank of TV lights. "I think the people of America will understand that."

Bush had concealed his arrest, but had he lied? That was the question reporters were asking. To conceal might simply be prudent, but to lie was to reveal an aspect of character. And in the rules of journalism, a candidate's character is fair game.

Although Bush had fended off questions about his past with a vague reference to youthful indiscretions, on one occasion he specifically denied being arrested. In an interview in 1998, Wayne Slater asked whether he had been arrested other than for stealing a

Christmas wreath as a college student. Bush said no, and then appeared to reconsider his answer, indicating he had more to say. But
Hughes cut him off. The reporter suggested that if Bush had something more to tell, he ought to tell it now, not risk having it emerge
at an inopportune time in some future campaign.

After Bush withstood the barrage of questions outside the cattle
barn and the media retreated to file its stories, everyone gathered at
the hotel for the night. The luggage had not yet arrived and Hughes
ordered a glass of wine as she waited.

"I know," she said, turning to the reporter. "You say we should
have gotten this out before now."

One of the rules of politics is to release the bad stuff on your
terms, not allow your opponents to do it on theirs. Hughes had violated that rule.

Hughes said she shut off the exchange between Bush and the reporter because she didn't know where the conversation was going.

"The governor was talking and winking at you, and I didn't
know what was going on. I don't think I knew then."

When Bush did tell her about the arrest, they made the decision
not to make the matter public.

Bush understood the potential political damage of his drunken-
driving arrest. He had already headed off public disclosure of the arrest once. Two years earlier, when the governor was summoned to
jury duty in 1996, Bush and his general counsel, Alberto Gonzales,
took steps to keep the episode secret. Publicly, the governor pro-
nounced himself eager to fulfill his obligation of citizenship by
serving on a jury. Privately, Gonzales met in chambers with the
judge and the attorney for the accused and urged that Bush be
stricken from the jury pool. The case involved a drunken-driving
charge and the defense attorney in the case said he was eager to
question the governor under oath about his "young and irresponsi-
ble" years. Gonzales moved quickly to head off such a prospect.

In chambers, Gonzales raised an ingenious legal argument: putting Bush on the jury would be a conflict of interest. Governors, he

argued, should not be deciding the fate of people in legal cases in which they might eventually be called on to consider pardons. The judge agreed and dismissed Bush from jury duty.

Even with the judge's action, some evidence of Bush's 1976 arrest still might have become public had the governor completely filled out a questionnaire required of potential jurors. The document asked "Have you ever been accused, or a complainant, or a witness in a criminal case?" The space was left blank. A spokesperson said later that an aide had filled out the document and didn't know the answer. Whatever the reason, the episode remained secret.

Gonzales' legal work won high praise from Bush. The young attorney had come from one of the powerful Houston law firms with Rove's blessing and with strong recommendations from influential business interests. Bush was impressed by Gonzales' intellect and conservative politics. The governor named him secretary of state in 1997 and, a year later, to an open seat on the Texas Supreme Court. Gonzales was bright, accomplished and Hispanic—Exactly the credentials rove knew would help expand the appeal of the Republican Party. When Gonzales ran for election to a full term on the state's high court, Rove made sure that business interests contributed several hundred thousand dollars to assure victory. When Bush went to the White House, he took Gonzales with him as general counsel. He later became U.S. attorney general and a figure of great controversy for a memo he wrote about Geneva Convention strictures against torture. Gonzales described them as "quaint."

Both Gonzales and Hughes had been successful keeping the lid on Bush's arrest while he was governor, but now the episode had burst full-force into public view in the final days of the presidential race. Now it was up to Karen Hughes alone.

Hughes had an unassailable integrity in dealing with the media, but her first loyalty was to Bush and her natural instinct was to protect him. The morning after word of the arrest leaked, she worked to tamp down the story, which was shifting from one of concealment to one of credibility. On the airplane, Hughes first suggested

Bush's remarks in 1998 had been off the record, then said Bush didn't remember making them at all—at least not as the reporter recalled them.

When the plane landed in Grand Rapids, Bush took the stage in the basketball arena of a Christian college and offered an oblique mea culpa to a cheering crowd of supporters.

"It's become clear to America over the course of this campaign that I've made mistakes in my life. But I'm proud to tell you, I've learned from those mistakes."

Journalists churned the drunken-driving story for another day, exploring Bush's effort to conceal the episode and questioning whether he'd been completely honest about it, but in the absence of new developments, the story ran dry and the media moved on. On the plane, the ever-ebullient Bush approached the reporter and laughed. "You ran me through the paces," he said.

Election Day was now less than 100 hours away. There was some evidence in the polling that the race was now tightening, but Team Bush was confident it had weathered the storm.

Now Rove was back, joining the campaign the final Sunday in Florida.

"I'm out!" he declared, bursting into the breakfast room at the hotel in Jacksonville where the media were having early-morning coffee. "They've let me out of the cage."

Rove had done the math and was pleased with his answer. He predicted that Bush would beat Gore by six percentage points with 320 electoral votes, 50 more than needed to win the White House.

"Could you lose?" a reporter asked.

Rove paused.

"We could lose," he said slowly, as if considering the possibility for a fleeting moment, then flashed a confident smile and repeated his prediction of victory.

As it turned out, Rove was wrong, at least in the short term. For all his skill, sometimes the numbers betrayed him. He had been wrong about New Hampshire in the primary and was wrong about winning California in the general election, squandering time and money better spent elsewhere. He engaged in the campaign too late in Minnesota and Wisconsin. And he was wrong about Election Day.

But he was right about West Virginia, and his decision to campaign there in a state with a history of nearly unflinching Democratic support; without West Virginia there would have been no recount in Florida and without Florida, no 5–4 decision by the U.S. Supreme Court. Florida was mostly a legal fight with James Baker III leading the effort, although Rove did help provide some political ground troops and did monitor affairs from headquarters in Austin and from a makeshift transition office opened in suburban Washington to give the impression during the legal fight that the outcome was inevitable. In the end, Rove did not win as planned, but he did win. After 36 days in Florida and 18 months on the road and a decade of planning and a lifetime of expectation—finally, Karl Christian Rove made it to the White House.

With Bush's victory as president, the "Iron Triangle" that had long competed for Bush's ear—Rove and Hughes and Allbaugh—headed for Washington. Rove and Hughes landed jobs in the West Wing; Allbaugh, whose wife was a lobbyist, was placed elsewhere at the Federal Emergency Management Agency.

Within two years, two of three loyalists who made up the triangle, announced they were leaving. Hughes was the first, saying she was moving back home to Austin where she would offer her advice from long distance. Then Joe Allbaugh announced he was quitting to set up a consulting firm offering advice on how to do business in war-torn Iraq. Rove was not the instrument of their departure, but the result was still the same—only Rove remained for the 2002 midterm elections as the architect of a historic Republican sweep, then the mastermind of a subsequent coup in the Senate that dislodged Trent Lott and put a close Bush ally in charge.

As the year ended, the *New York Times* reported, "President Bush has created one of the most powerful White Houses in at least a generation, prominent Democrats and Republicans say."

With Mr. Bush's allies in place on Capitol Hill, "the president has consolidated what even Democrats say is a stunning degree of authority in the White House at the halfway point of his four-year term. The perception that Mr. Bush and his chief political counsel, Karl Rove, orchestrated a coup in the Senate—not withstanding the official White House denials that it had anything to do with Senator Trent Lott's decision on Friday to give up his leadership post— has only enhanced what veteran political strategists say is the political potency of the White House."

Back home in Austin, long-time political ally David Weeks was not surprised by Rove's ascension to power.

"I always said from the day he got to Washington, he'd own it."

15

Rovian Cancer

A patriot must always be ready to defend his country from
his government.

—Edward Abbey

K arl Rove's intentions and his strategies are never understandable until the conclusion of political events. The
truth is always subtext. Rove's use of language is unique
because he manages to communicate without directly
addressing his subject matter. After the fact, when the president
has decided to invade Iraq or change environmental regulations,
Rove's words from the previous six months suddenly take on a heft
they lacked when he was talking around the issue. Rove speaks of
right and wrong, hope and progress, but he is communicating
money and power wrapped in a robe of morality.

Morality is the costume his politics wears.

And it is also the guise Rove gave the president to use in dealing
with Iraq. His standard of behavior is different when comparing Iraq
and, for example, Cuba. Cuba must change from within, an eventu-
ality caused by the suffering of the Cuban people, who Rove insists

are obligated to overthrow Fidel Castro. For Iraq, Rove applies a different standard and envisioned a revolution that will arrive in the form of U.S. Army battalions and laser-guided bombs. Of course, Cuba does not sit astride the world's second largest known reserves of oil. Iraq does. And Cuba is not a threat to Israel, one of the United States' closest allies. Rove's America was not willing to wait for the people of Iraq to turn out Saddam.

"Iraq has developed and acquired from the North Koreans and expanded its ability to deliver weapons in the region, whether it's Ankara, or Tel Aviv, or Riyadh, or the oil fields," Rove said. "All of these things are now within easy distance of his intermediate range weapons. We've got a bad actor. We've got a really bad actor."

However bad he was, Hussein did not possess the weapons of mass destruction Rove and the White House claimed and the evidence indicates they were aware of that fact from the time they began banging the drums of war. Nonetheless, Rove knows what he wants. He knows what the president wants. He knows what the U.S. military wants. And he knows what corporate America wants. His job is sharply defined as creating a political climate that turns those wants into the public's demand. Keeping it simple does that. We are good. Iraq is bad. We love freedom. They do not. A clear, accessible message for an electorate too busy to read deeper into the story. The language must not be bloody. It's regime change. Not war. Clean and antiseptic. More of a procedure than a battle.

It's a bad thing that Saddam has all that oil.

But for Rove's political goals, it's a good thing that Saddam is such a bad man.

"Here's a guy who has been actively pursuing, for the better part of two decades, radiological, biological, chemical, and nuclear weapons," Rove argued. "There's very strong belief, absent the Israeli raid on the reactor, that he was within a couple of years of developing nuclear. We don't know. At least the people who do know aren't saying."

Of course, those claims weren't true. But that did not change the political power that was accessed simply by making the allegations. Nothing had changed about Rove's ideas. Saddam was still the Bush White House's bad guy. They needed a substitute because Osama was elusive. Saddam was just sitting there, buoyed on a sea of oil. He wasn't the evildoer they wanted. But Saddam would serve the current purpose. And the most critical part of that was using the war in Iraq for acquiring political dominance in Washington. The Republicans wanted to control the U.S. Congress. The party was looking to Karl to show them the way. He was expected to develop a strategy that would defy history and he intended to do precisely that. Karl Rove was always the man with the plan.

But he was also a part of another plan.

And this time it wasn't his. The terrorist attacks of September 11 had created a new environment for polices that were once considered radical. Rove's strategy for Election Day 2002 and for the president's reelection in 2004 was aimed at building support for these new policies. The plan was already being rolled out on a global stage but it would be harder to execute without Republican power and a mandate for the president. But that was okay. Rove could handle the responsibility. What he liked about politics was that everything was a contest. He liked a good fight. A tough race. A contest.

And no contest had greater stakes than war.

On the campaign to the White House, Rove had made sure his client kept the electorate assured they were not going to be in any military and political tar pits overseas. George W. Bush frequently told crowds his would not be "an administration that gets involved in nation building" and that, if the United States sent troops anywhere, "I won't let it happen without an exit strategy." But America was attacked. And suddenly President Bush was nation building in Afghanistan. U.S. forces invaded Iraq and no one in the White House discusses an exit strategy. Because there is none. A new world appears to be taking form. And Rove is an instrument of its creation.

Karl Rove had become the man with someone else's plan.

Except the war on terrorism wasn't going so well.

Osama bin Laden was invisible. The most powerful government in the world was unable to find a six-foot, four-inch tall, bearded Muslim, who's on dialysis, clanking around attached to medical equipment. U.S. intelligence didn't even know if the chief evildoer was alive or dead after the attack on Afghanistan. Tapes purporting to contain his face and voice were surfacing and appeared both real and untraceable. Bin Laden was almost incorporeal, slipping across borders undetected, taunting the U.S. military and the American president. Meanwhile, suicide bombers were keep attacking Israelis and other U.S. allies.

Very little progress was being made. A few top al-Qaeda operatives were taken into custody. But not their leader. U.S. intelligence agencies kept getting mixed signals about potential attacks against Americans. Alarming warnings were issued and then retracted or revised. Americans were getting uneasy. No one had any real sense of what to expect. How do you fight an enemy you cannot see? The president could claim progress but was unable to prove it. The public believed in George W. Bush but it did not like the way things were going. And this discontent was rising as the fall elections loomed. Unchecked, these kinds of sentiments had the potential to harm the president and his party's hopes of gaining power in Congress.

Karl Rove needed a better, simpler, more marketable war than something as vague as the war on terrorism.

A political operative who has closely observed Rove's tactics for many years described the rationale Rove employed for what was coming next.

"What if we haven't avenged the Twin Towers? How do the president and Rove not suffer from that? And it was starting to look like we couldn't win the war on terrorism. Rather than lose that war we redefine that war. Suddenly it wasn't the people who were terrorists who killed us. It was evil itself. They can apply that to anyone they want. Tom Daschle or Hussein."

And this approach melded nicely with an agenda Vice President Dick Cheney and Deputy Secretary of Defense Paul Wolfowitz had been pushing for a decade to expand American influence and military abroad into a form of empire. Rove's political strategy for the president transformed a policy whose scope and tenets were unprecedented in American history.

All it needed was a little justification.

And Iraq was handy.

Karl Rove got to work. And he came up with a strategy that provided a turnkey solution to every crisis President Bush was confronting. The Democratic advantage went away overnight.

Jason Stanford, a national Democratic consultant who operates out of Texas, admitted his side was politically disarmed by Rove's ingenuity.

"It was just brilliant. They figured out real soon that Osama was going to be a hard guy to go and get. He can hide in a cave, right? So, what do they do? They just picked a war they could win. Hey, we can't take over a country that doesn't exist, so fine we'll go take over some country. We can't invade al Qaeda. We can't occupy it. We can't even find it. Okay. Fine. But we do know where Baghdad is. We've got a map. We can find it on a map. And they've got oil and an evil guy. So let's go there. They never stop and say that. But they know it's what they are doing. It has to be the most evil political calculation in American history."

A simplification but the rudiments of a plan.

Karl Rove did not, however, wake up one bright morning and say, "I've got it, Mr. President. If you'll just invade Iraq, we can take care of all of your domestic problems on the economy, corporate corruption, unkept campaign promises, and the war on terrorism." There was, though, a political judgment made about making Iraq the object of our national anger. We weren't just taking on terrorism. We were confronting evil itself. And, clearly, Saddam was evil and, as such, he was nothing more than a terrorist in charge of a country.

Arguments were easy to make, whether substantive or not, that he likely helped the Arabs who attacked on 9/11.

Demonstrably, though, what had Saddam Hussein done to suddenly be moved up on the list of bad guys? In the decade since U.S. forces routed Iraqi troops from Kuwait, Baghdad had been dealing with poverty, disease, a deteriorating infrastructure, and a hopeless economy in spite of an abundance of oil. Even the Central Intelligence Agency, in a 2002 report to Congress, said it was unable to offer evidence Saddam was connected to Islamic terrorists or was developing weapons of mass destruction. Containment and deterrence had worked with Iraq. Saddam feared doing anything rash because he knew retribution was certain to be swift and complete. His behavior had largely been consistent since the conclusion of the Persian Gulf War. Certainly not good. But not as evil as the White House needed him to be. The "Suddenly Saddam" strategy came out of nowhere. President Bush barely mentioned the Iraqi dictator to the public when he was running for office. Nothing about Saddam had changed significantly in more than 10 years.

The initial expression of this new thinking occurred the first day of June as the president spoke to the graduating class of cadets at West Point. In a commencement address, whose contextual importance was largely missed by the media, Bush's language revealed that deterrence had been abandoned as U.S. military policy. When reporters did not play the story prominently, the White House had staffers go out and re-spin the news. A single word, used only once in the text of the president's speech, characterized its important, underlying message: preemption.

"I will not stand by as peril grows closer and closer," the president told his West Point audience. "If we wait for threats to fully materialize, we will have waited too long."

"The war on terror will not be won on the defensive"

"We cannot defend America and our friends by hoping for the best."

The language was unmistakable and not subject to interpretation. The president was informing the wider world that America was assuming the office of global sheriff. There were good guys and bad guys. We were going after the bad guys. And anyone who did not think like America was very likely an enemy. Looking and acting suspiciously were now sufficient grounds for the United States to seek you out as an enemy of freedom and democracy. We were no longer waiting for trouble as a motive for intervention.

Due process is limited in this new American internationalism.

"All of a sudden," one Democrat suggested, "we're the cowboy who walked into the saloon with a gun, saying, 'get behind me if you're with me or we're gonna shoot ya.'"

The president had also laid his predicate for acting against Iraq. Suspicions were now enough, even if intelligence efforts were unable to substantiate allegations against Saddam. The ensuing debate over acting preemptively against Iraq, the timing of the public discourse and the moments of great decision, all show the trademarks of a disciplined campaign run by Karl Rove.

The Democrats, though, caught on too late.

Jim Jordan, the director of the Democratic Senatorial Campaign Committee, was considered prescient for comments he made in August 2002 as he was briefing political reporters. Energized by the war on terrorism having grown quiet, and Wall Street acting equally drowsy, Jordan felt Democrats would benefit from politics moving back to the pocketbooks of voters. Jordan said he thought something was happening in the American electorate and that it would accrue to the benefit of his party. But he was asked if he thought Republicans might regain political dominance over the agenda with the issues of terrorism and war.

His answer was widely quoted.

"You mean when General Rove calls in the air strikes in October?"

As cynical as the remark may have sounded, it had an underlying logic. Jordan, recognizing he had shocked a few people in his audience, added, "I hope I'm wrong. Certainly, none of us want to think that the administration, for domestic political reasons, would use the war. But I think the temptation will be strong."

The calculated nature of what Rove and his president were doing was revealed in a *New York Times* article quoting Chief of Staff Andy Card. Card indicated the White House was resisting launching its public relations offensive on Iraq because, "from a marketing point of view, you don't introduce new products in August."

And so they did not.

But when Congress returned, Bush and Rove began to take control of the national debate by stepping up efforts to pressure Congress for a resolution authorizing the use of force against Iraq. The Democrats knew, immediately, Rove had them co-opted. War on terrorism had previously been declared, so effectively, the United States was already in a state of war. If the president had also identified Iraq as an enemy, any member of Congress who resisted the Iraqi resolution was in danger of appearing to not support the president in a time of national peril. Not a good place to be, politically. Unfortunately, the dominating characteristic of Democratic Party leaders was cowardice at the time of that debate, including future presidential candidate John Kerry.

However, the options for Democrats were perplexing. A lengthy debate in Congress, to clarify why the Iraqi resolution was foolish, would have the effect of covering up discussion of domestic issues, where Democrats had the edge. The political conundrum was proof that Rove had them outflanked. If Democrats helped to pass the resolution quickly, there was a chance that they could execute a political return to domestic affairs like the economy, corporate corruption, health care, and even pension reform. But the president still had a chance to keep eyes on the Iraqi controversy by pursuing a joint resolution before the United Nations. Between the United Nations and Congress, war talk with Iraq could be timed to fill the entire fall campaign schedule.

As Congress haggled over the syntax and importance of an Iraq resolution, the president addressed members in joint session to talk about possible war with Iraq and unveil his new National Security

Strategy. Affirming the ideas first espoused at West Point, the president gave U.S. foreign policy an evolutionary shove to the right by
claiming America was justified in striking preemptively against perceived enemies.

Now we were relying on perception, not proof, preemption instead of deterrence.

"The greater the threat, the greater is the risk of inaction," the
president said. "And the more compelling the case for taking antici-
patory action to defend ourselves, even if uncertainty remains as to
the time and place of the enemy's attack. To forestall or prevent such
hostile acts by our adversaries, the United States will, if necessary,
act preemptively."

Making the case for war against Iraq was not easy, unless you ju-
diciously avoided the facts. The president filled his campaign
speeches with fears that Saddam Hussein was on the verge of acquiring a nuclear weapon while the esteemed International Institute
for Strategic Studies reported that Iraq was years away from developing a bomb of its own. The White House also conveniently ignored the fact that radical Islamists like the al Qaeda viewed Saddam
with almost as much loathing as they did America. His regime is sec-
ular, not Islamist and that makes him the enemy of al Qaeda. A member of a minority sect of Islam, the Sunnis, Saddam has no reason to
conspire with the terrorists who attacked the United States. Getting
rid of Saddam will do nothing to alleviate terrorist threats to America, and presidential rhetoric cannot change that.

As he campaigned around the country for Republican candidates, Karl Rove kept the president lasered onto the message. The
world was a dangerous place. Saddam was only one of many despots
America needed to confront. Bush's National Security Strategy, jus-
tifying preemptive action, was a bold template for dealing with the
new threats. Voters appeared disinterested in domestic concerns and
did not bother with envisioning where the president's policy of preemption might take their country.

But there were reasons to tremble. Even among conservatives.

Writing in Patrick Buchanan's *The American Conservative*, Paul W. Schroeder argued that, instead of stabilizing international politics, the president was about to make the planet a more tremulous and worried place with the concept of preemption.

"The American example and standard for preemptive war, if carried out, would invite imitation and emulation, and get it. One can easily imagine plausible scenarios in which India could justify attacking Pakistan, or vice versa, or Israel any one of its neighbors, or China Taiwan, or South Korea North Korea, under this rule that suspicion of what a hostile regime might do justifies launching preemptive wars to overthrow it."

A conservative on the far right, Schroeder did not sound very different from Gore Vidal on the left, who posted a 7,000-word deconstruction of the new Bush doctrine in the *London Observer.*

Regardless of the dubious policy, the president's popularity did not falter. Everywhere he went, adoring crowds gathered to hear him speak for Republican candidates in the 2002 mid-term elections. Karl Rove scheduled Bush into numerous locations where the GOP needed to win. And under the cover of war, nothing the president said seemed to cause him political harm. When he suggested during an East Coast trip that the Senate was holding up the Homeland Security bill because it was not "as interested in the safety and security of the American people as it needed to be," there ought to have been greater outrage and political backlash. Senator Daniel Inouye of Hawaii had known the darkness of war from World War II and Senator Max Cleland of Georgia, who had left two legs and an arm in Vietnam, both failed to speak in a public and personal manner about the president's insult. The man who had criticized them escaped combat in Vietnam by getting a coveted slot in a "champagne" unit of the Texas Air National Guard.

As the president logged tens of thousands of miles on Air Force One, executing the Karl Rove midterm strategy, he appeared politically invincible. Using his popularity acquired through the War on Terrorism, Rove had the president concentrate on the threat posed by Hussein. Unflagging in his verbal attacks on Iraq, Bush expressed certitude, a confidence of cause, which drew people to him and his party's candidates. Americans like a president who can make decisions and believe in himself.

Karl Rove understood the political value of this key Bush characteristic.

"I've seen, even in this White House, I've seen people agonizing over decisions, but I've never seen him," Rove said.

The presidential advisor claimed Bush told him, during a private meeting in the Oval Office, that he has not regretted a single decision he has made since 9/11.

"So, I thought about it afterwards, because, you know, history is really littered with people who agonized over decisions, even great presidents sometimes found themselves agonizing over decisions, and I'm sure there will be some moments where there's a decision he'll agonize over, but you don't want a president who walks into the Oval Office every morning and says, 'Oh god, I've got to make decisions,' because that's what the job is all about."

The sense of being absolutely correct is a dangerous trait, especially when a president has a political advisor who edits the information used to arrive at decisions. In the case of Bush, it is made more treacherous by a president who dislikes data overload. During one particular staff meeting, Bush is reported to have told his advisors that they were "nuancing him to death."

"Checking a box decisively is a nice thing," said political scientist Bruce Buchanan. "Especially compared to wringing your hands endlessly, like Clinton did. But if it's a process where the deck is stacked in advance and you know what box is going to be checked, decisively wrong doesn't strike me as that much of an advantage over being confusedly right."

If only North Korea had not made the decision on the Iraqi crisis look silly and manufactured.

North Korea's leader Kim Jong-il acknowledged to the United States that his country had a maturing nuclear weapons program. And he told the president as Congress was debating the Iraq resolution. The timing was worse than even the hypocrisies the news made of the White House policy toward Iraq. How was North Korea less dangerous than Saddam? Kim had the long-range missiles to deliver nuclear warheads. Pyongyang had violated a 1994 weapons agreement by developing nuclear capabilities. According to the Washington Post, the president's own language may have prompted the violation. A source told the newspaper "the North Koreans decided to go ahead with the [nuclear] program after President Bush identified them as a member of the international axis of evil."

The strategy the White House used to deal with this troubling news appears to have come from the mind of Karl Rove. First intelligence reports on North Korea's nuclear assets reached the Bush administration during the summer, as efforts were being made to clarify support and causes for the war against Iraq. But the White House kept quiet. When Kim formally confirmed to Washington, through normal diplomatic channels, that he had nuclear strength, Congress was in the midst of debating the resolution demanding Saddam disarm or face the consequences.

But the White House kept the news from Congress for 12 days, until the debate on Iraq was closed.

Such a move is the political equivalent of holding up a sign reading, "Karl was here."

But the Democrats had no voice. No one expressed indignation with the White House's behavior, even though there was an abundance of questions worth asking. Democrats could hardly campaign against a war they had helped to declare. And no one has ever gotten elected by running against a tax cut, in spite of the fact that the Bush reductions mostly benefited corporations and the wealthy.

Democrats were cornered by Karl.

The campaign was brilliant.

The president swirled in and out of 15 states identified by Karl Rove as crucial to Republican gains in Congress for 2002. Bush was almost mythological, descending from the sky in the world's command center called Air Force One, possessed of a relentless level of approval from the people who were enduring hard times caused, in part, by his leadership. In the closing days, it was obvious voters were deciding to give the president what he wanted: congressional control for Republicans and a mandate to clear out Saddam.

"It is almost eerie, what Rove has done," one Washington consultant said. "He dismantled the Democrats so effectively they just stood there, dumbstruck. He silenced their opposition with intimidation, picked apart institutions, just basically destroyed dissent, and he wrapped all of this in patriotic hues. I'm telling you, it's scarily phenomenal."

The Republicans won the 2002 battle by obscuring the domestic issues with Iraq and terrorism, just as Karl Rove had advised almost a year earlier. They used it again for effective leverage in the 2004 reelection campaign and tossed in gay marriage issues to close the deal with conservatives. But Rove knew the truth about the Bush policy toward Iraq in both races. He simply ignored it. Just as the Democrats stood back, afraid to speak about what was unfolding.

There was one person who articulated the facts. Of course, Karl Rove had him cornered, too. No one was listening to Iraqi foreign minister Tareq Aziz because he worked for Saddam Hussein and had been complicit in the Iraqi dictator's crimes of slaughtering and torturing his own people. But in one, short sentence, he captured the issues no American politician had the courage to confront.

"This," he said, "is all about oil and Israel."

No one who knows Karl Rove has been surprised to hear his name as a prime suspect in the scandal involving the leak of a CIA agent's name. This is how Karl Rove has operated in the political arena for his entire career. If he had an Achilles' heel as an operative, it was only his temper. When crossed, Rove's anger was legendary, and was always manifest in the tactics he deployed to exact retribution against those who he felt had wronged him. The greater shock for Washington, and journalists who have reported on

Karl Rove's career, would be if he were not involved in outing undercover agent Valerie Plame.

Back in Texas, one of Rove's early political victims has always worried about how power might magnify Rove's already frighteningly adept political skills. Pete McRae went to prison for being only marginally associated with the kind of political work that takes place in Texas politics every day. An allegedly Rove-fueled investigation, conducted by an overeager FBI agent, convicted McRae and Deputy Agriculture Commissioner Mike Moeller of, essentially, not being very good supervisors. They got 18 months in federal penitentiaries.

"I've always worried about what Karl might do with real power," McRae said. "When you have a guy like this, and he has the power of the entire U.S. government at his disposal, I think you can expect some unsavory things to take place. Look at what he got done while he was nothing more than a campaign manager for an unknown candidate from rural Texas."

A close study of what has happened since Karl Rove arrived in Washington will show he has not changed his behavior, nor has his level of influence on the president diminished. It has, in fact, increased dramatically with both politics and policy now an official part of his portfolio. Karl Rove is simply painting on a larger canvas, and doing so with the same eye for detail that marked his rise in Texas.

In the case of Ambassador Joseph Wilson, all of the "Karl Rove Has Been Here" signs are scattered up and down the thoroughfare of that scandal. In the rationale of Rove, it was okay for Wilson to travel to Niger to check and see if Saddam Hussein and Iraq had tried to purchase yellowcake uranium. This was not Wilson's sin. The ambassador agitated Rove when he did not keep his mouth shut about his findings. Wilson reported his conclusion using proper protocol and governmental channels to both the CIA and the State Department. And he assumed, wrongly, that was the end of the affair. There was no basis to the Niger uranium claims. The documents purportedly showing the purchase were proved false, and rather easily.

The administration, presumably with Rove's guidance, had been very effective at putting a cap on intelligence that contradicted Bush Administration allegations about Hussein's efforts to acquire weapons of mass destruction. Vice President Dick Cheney, often with former Congressman Newt Gingrich in tow, met almost daily with intelligence officials at CIA headquarters in Langley, Virginia. Analysts have said that it was made clear to them, whenever they delivered reports that contradicted what the White House wanted, they were given the unmistakable message to go back and look for what was "really" there.

"They wanted us to cook it," one operative said.

Faced with intimidation, a tactic Rove cultivated for the Bush administration, people who actually knew the truth about Iraq's armaments, or lack thereof, were never allowed to come forth. This is how a shipment of aluminum tubes, marked by an Italian rocket manufacturer as a "Medusa 81" rocket body, were redefined as casings for a uranium gas centrifuge. There was an abundance of contradictory intelligence on these tubes, which clearly proved they could not be used in the construction of a centrifuge, but that data was effectively suppressed.

Similar pressures were operating when Ambassador Wilson returned with his report. He, alone among all voices in the Washington bureaucracy, was willing to confront the truth. Shocked by the fact that the president included the Niger yellowcake lie into his State of the Union speech, Wilson wrote an opinion piece for the *New York Times*, which proved there was no substance to the claim. A week later, reporters were calling to ask about his wife's line of work. This is either great coincidence, or Karl Rove. Circumstantial, anecdotal, and historical evidence all point at the president's senior advisor.

Rove, as is his habit, denied any connections. However, a grand jury investigation was launched by one of the country's most tenacious prosecutors, Patrick Fitzgerald of Chicago, and the White House counsel may have contradicted himself during the inquiry.

Consistently, Rove told reporters that he never spoke to anyone
about CIA agent Valerie Plame until after her name had been published in a column by Robert Novak. But an e-mail written by *Time*
magazine's Matt Cooper indicated that Rove had been discussing
her before Novak's story was in print. Similar claims under oath to
either FBI investigators or a federal grand jury could lead to great
legal problems and potential criminal charges of perjury, if such allegations were provable in court.

Not surprisingly, journalists and political pros think Rove designed the leak strategy to blow the cover of Ambassador Wilson's
wife. The purpose of this, of course, was to keep the lid on anyone
who might want to also come out with contradictory intelligence,
embarrassing the White House. The message was that anyone who
messed with the Bush team might also find themselves and their
families living at risk. While the leak strategy is classic Rove, it's just
as likely he did not make the initial calls to reporters, though there
has been reporting that he made follow up contact with some journalists. He always puts a layer of operatives between himself and the
actual implementation of any plan of attack. All of the investigative
roads can be expected to lead back to Rove, but, if past practice is
any indication, they will wash out from a deluge of deception before
they get to their destination.

The shock value of this leak did not result from the fact that it
happened. What has proved astounding has been its blatant obvi-
ousness, the calculated meanness, the sort of business plan execution of disseminating the information. The Bush White House has
been virtually leak proof. Fierce loyalties to the president and Karl
Rove's absolute control have been credited for this characteristic.
No one would have dared to leak information on a CIA agent without getting Karl Rove to check the "yes" box on the plan. To believe
that Rove was oblivious to what happened requires complete aban-
donment of any knowledge of his past behavior in the arena of politics, or ignoring his comprehensive involvement in the most minute
of details in the Bush White House.

In a nation at war, the Bush White House, or a senior official within the Bush administration, both of which are completely dominated by Rove, has allowed an agent of the U.S. government to be exposed. Even if the perpetrator were not Rove, this is still a crime in the nation's most important public office. The fact that Valerie Plame has put her life at risk serving her country was apparently of no concern to the administration's leakers. Nor is the all too rich irony that she has been working in the area of weapons of mass destruction, undoubtedly having more impact on the safety and security of Americans than the Bush counselors who argued attacking Iraq would reduce our chances of being hit with WMD. If Rove is ever fingered as treasonous, he will argue that he had no idea that Valerie Plame was undercover. Even if a record of calls exists, it will not prove what was said. It will only show that he dialed up reporters.

Karl Rove will not go away.

President Bush cannot imagine a political life without Karl Rove. Even if the investigation of the leaks accumulates serious evidence against the senior advisor, the president will be more likely to build a protective wall around Rove than cut him loose. As maligned as the Bush intellect is, the president is smart to know the value of the people who got him elected. He knows there would be no second Bush presidency, if there were no planning, strategy, fund-raising, and nasty subterfuge choreographed by Karl Rove. If Rove were to ever be ousted from the Bush White House, it would require a confidante like Karen Hughes or Vice President Dick Cheney to convince the president that Rove was harming the administration and the GOP.

Meanwhile, the machinations of Rove will continue to confound journalism, politics, and international policy of the United States. In journalism, the leak has created a moral dilemma. There are reporters in Washington who can tell the FBI who called them with the leak. As soon as they do that, however, they will be finished in a town where the engines of journalism run on the gas from leaks. Fortunately, Rove has angered as many journalists as he has other political interests, and there is always the hope that, if he was the person who leaked, one of those reporters will adhere to a higher ethic than source protection. Identifying a traitor in a time of war, someone who has exposed his country to danger is of greater importance than a solitary career in journalism.

Writing about Rove often results in accusations that his influence is being wildly overstated. Unfortunately, Rove leaves behind nothing but ephemera for anyone trying to prove his power. But the language and policy of the White House has shown Roverian texture in every endeavor of the Bush administration. Americans love their presidents the most during crisis, thus, Iraq is just a battle in a larger war on terrorism. In terms of positioning, Rove has also guided the White House in describing the current occupation of Iraq as the battlefront in the war on terrorism. It wasn't, though, until America got there and began to provide handy targets to terrorists flocking into Iraq from around the Muslim world. Attacks on troops are consistently characterized as acts of terror, which, of course they are, and the American public is convincingly told that, "If we don't stop them there, we will face them in our own country." The national discourse, under Karl Rove's message guidance, and the White House's public relations campaign, is moving on from the lies and disingenuousness that led to the invasion. The purpose of the war seems to change almost daily and nothing beyond increased body counts is accomplished. A constitutional convention cannot reach consensus and a sectarian civil war appears more likely with each improvised explosive device.

As America moves through the second Bush term, few aspects of life in this country have not been affected by Karl Rove, and his profound influence on the president and his policies. He is the political mastermind of an administration that has preached compassionate conservatism, but has practiced something considerably different. If Karl Rove were not sitting in his office in the White House, there might have been no war in Iraq; there would be underprivileged children still attending Head Start programs, which have been reduced or eliminated; there would be low income families getting health care from the Children's Health Insurance Program, instead of going without because of federal cutbacks in funding; there would be competitive bidding on contracts to rebuild Iraq instead of delivery of deals to Halliburton and other companies that are GOP fund-raisers; there would have been no California recall; there would be congressional districts with lines drawn to help elect minorities; there would be a complete and honest report from the 9/11 Commission; there would be real accounting of Saudi Arabia's involvement in acts of terrorism; there would be real funding for Homeland Security's First Responders; there would even be more people with jobs; half of $87 billion requested for rebuilding Iraq might be used to implement full coverage health care for every man, woman, and child in America.

And sadly, none of this is overstatement.

Notes

Introduction: King Karl or Mr. Co-President?

Page 1   "'I think he's . . .'" Bruce Buchanan interview, University of Texas (2000).

Page 2   "'The politics at the . . .'" Author interview with Rove (Austin, 2002).

Page 4   "'We're a group . . .'" Author interview with Rove (Austin, 2002).

Page 4   "The duties keep . . ." *Wall Street Journal* (August 2002).

Page 5   "'Yeah, I think he's . . .'" interview with Mauro (Austin, 2002).

Page 5   "Jim Hightower, the Democratic . . ." *Dallas Morning News* (February 1990).

Page 6   "Unfortunately, the political bullet . . ." *Dallas Morning News* (September 1993).

Page 7   "An amateur historian . . ." American Enterprise Institute, Rove seminar (December 2001).

Chapter 1: Off to the Show

Page 12   "'Karl just dominates . . .'" interview with Republican anonymous source.

Page 13   "And among Bush family . . ." *New York Times* (March 2000).

Page 15   "'The playing field . . .'" interview with anonymous Democratic source.

Chapter 2: Consultant, Bug Thyself

Page 18   "For almost seven . . ." FBI incident report (October 10, 1986).

Page 18   "Gary L. Morphew . . ." Texas Department of Public Safety incident report, October 7, 1986.

Page 19   "'It wouldn't surprise me . . .'" FBI incident report (October 10, 1986).

Page 19   "'There have been a number . . .'" *Houston Chronicle* (October 12, 1986).

Page 19   "'I'm not picking up . . .'" FBI incident report (October 10, 1986).

Page 19   "Scott said that . . ." FBI incident report (October 10, 1986).

Page 19   "This time, Scott . . ." FBI incident report (October 10, 1986).

Page 19   "The bug was found . . ." Texas Department of Public Safety incident report (October 7, 1986).

Page 20   "'Turn it off . . .'" *Austin American-Statesman* (October 12, 1986).

Page 20   "Morphew said he told . . ." *Austin American-Statesman* (October 12, 1986).

Page 20   "According to Texas . . ." Texas Department of Public Safety incident report (October 7, 1986).

Page 20   "In the interim, . . ." FBI incident report (October 10, 1986).

Page 21   "'ROVE AND CLEMENTS . . .'" FBI incident report (October 10, 1986).

Page 21   "'Checking my office . . .'" Author interview with Rove (Austin, August 2002).

Page 22   "'Are you sure . . .'" Author interview with Rove (Austin, August 2002).

Page 23   "After reporters arrived . . ." author present at event.

Page 23   "'Obviously, I do not know . . .'" *Austin American-Statesman* (October 7, 1986).

Page 23   "'How do we know . . .'" KPRC-TV report.

Page 25   "'I don't know anything . . .'" *Dallas Morning News* (October 8, 1986).

Page 25   "'Mark White got word . . .'" Author interview with Alofsin (August 2002).

Page 26   "'If they found a bug . . .'" *Austin American-Statesman* (October 8, 1986).

Page 26   "'Whoever thought . . .'" *Houston Chronicle* (October 12, 1986).

Chapter 3: Politically Paranormal

Page 28   "'And we got this . . .'" interview with Republican anonymous source.

Page 28   "'I told them to do . . .'" *Dallas Morning News* (October 13, 1986).

Page 28   "'I removed that device . . .'" FBI incident report, October 10, 1986.

Page 28   "'I have no legal . . .'" *Austin American-Statesman* (October 1986).

Page 29   "'I can tell you . . .'" *Austin American-Statesman* (October 19, 1986).

Page 29   "Results of the FBI lab . . ." FBI incident report.

Page 29   "'It seems to me . . .'" *Houston Chronicle* (October 1986).

Page 29   "'I don't know why . . .'" *Austin American-Statesman* (October 1986).

Page 30   "'Why didn't they just . . .'" *Houston Chronicle* (October 1986).

Page 30   "'Later that day . . .'" Author interview with Rove (August 2002).

Page 31   "When he was interviewed . . ." FBI incident report.

Page 31   "'We haven't placed a buy . . .'" Author interview with Rove (August 2002).

Page 31   "'DIAMOND ADVISED THAT . . .'" FBI incident report.

Page 32   "IT APPEARS THAT . . ." FBI incident report.

Page 33   "'I wouldn't quite call it . . .'" Davis interview (July 2002).

Page 33   "'Did Karl know . . .'" Republican anonymous source interview.

Page 33   "'We were completely aware . . .'" FBI anonymous source interview.

Page 34   "'I have no idea . . .'" Author interview with Rove (August 2002).

Page 34   "'The numbers show . . .'" McKinnon interview (August 2002).

Page 34   "Rarely chatty with . . ." *New York Times* (March 14, 2000).

Page 35   "The movie showed up . . ." *New York Times* (March 2000).

Page 35   "'That's why it was . . .'" Author interview with Rove (August 2002).

Page 36   "'Of course, Rove knew . . .'" Author interview with Alofsin (August 2002).

Page 36   "'I don't remember . . .'" Author interview with Alofsin (August 2002).

Chapter 4: Livin' with the Long Knives

Page 39   "He had called the . . ." *Austin American-Statesman* (August 11, 1991).

Page 40   "Although USDA's internal . . ." USDA letter to Larry Beauchamp (November 2, 1989).

Page 40   "Before joining the Travis County . . ." Beauchamp resume, job application to Travis County District Attorney (March 2, 1987).

Page 40   "Beauchamp had become . . ." *Austin American-Statesman* (August 11, 1991).

Page 40   "'To question my . . .'" *Austin American-Statesman* (August 11, 1991).

Page 41   "When asked by a reporter . . ." *Austin American-Statesman* (August 11, 1990).

Page 42   "'At that time . . .'" Pete McRae interview (July 2002).

Page 42   "The next morning . . ." USDA letter to Larry Beauchamp (November 2, 1989).

Page 42   "'And I furnished him . . .'" *Austin American-Statesman* (August 11, 1990).

Page 43   "'I'd heard about . . .'" interview with Buck Wood (July 2002).

Page 43   "'He showed up in . . .'" interview with Garry Mauro (July 2002).

Page 43   "'You gotta understand . . .'" interview with Garry Mauro (July 2002).

Page 43   "'You think Rove . . .'" interview with Garry Mauro (July 2002).

Page 44   "Byron Sage, the special . . ." Byron Sage interview (July 2002).

Page 44   "But assistant U.S. attorney . . ." Jesse Oliver interview, based on conversation between Oliver and TDA defense attorney's phone call with Mills.

Page 44   "According to Tomaso's story . . ." *Dallas Morning News* (October 31, 1989).

Page 45   "'In terms of how it worked . . .'" Jesse Oliver interview.

Page 45   "'I can't tell you for . . .'" David Elliot interview (July 2002).

Page 45   "The headline was . . ." *Dallas Morning News* (November 13, 1989).

Page 45   "The chief fund-raiser . . ." Moeller, McRae, Oliver interviews, Texas Secretary of State records.

Page 46   "'I actually engineered . . .'" McRae interview.

Page 46   "They did their fund-raising . . ." Moeller, McRae, Quicksall trial court testimony; Moeller, McRae interviews.

Page 46   "Boyd and Koontz intended . . ." Moeller, McRae, Oliver interviews; court documents.

Page 46   "Tomaso's story that . . ." *Dallas Morning News* (November 13, 1990).

Page 46   "'If he is not . . .'" *Dallas Morning News* (November 13, 1990).

Page 47   "Reporters, like Debbie Graves . . ." Moeller, McRae, Oliver interviews.

Page 47   "'I do know that I became . . .'" Texas State Senate Rove testimony (March 26, 1991).

Page 48   "'I don't recall . . .'" Texas State Senate Rove testimony (March 26, 1991).

Page 49   "'I can't remember . . .'" Texas State Senate Rove testimony (March 26, 1991).

Page 49   "'This summer [1990] I met with agent . . .'" U.S. Senate, Committee on Foreign Relations, sworn affidavit to Board for International Broadcasting (August 27, 1990).

Page 49   "While charging that their agency . . ." Texas State Auditor's final report on Texas-Federal Inspection Service (December 1, 1989).

Page 50   "The day the report . . ." McRae, Jesse Oliver interviews.

Page 50   "'We were drinking . . .'" McRae interview.

Page 50   "'That was the pivotal thought . . .'" Oliver interview.

Chapter 5: Running for Cover

Page 51   "Before talking with reporters . . ." *Mineral Wells Index* (December 4, 1989).

Page 52   "'USDA officials are not . . .'" *Austin-American Statesman, Dallas Morning News* (December 6, 1989, various).

Page 52   "Unannounced, Rampton arrived . . ." Moeller, McRae, Oliver interviews, trial documents.

Page 52   "'I do know he played . . .'" Moeller interview.

Page 53   "'I will just tell you . . .'" Author interview with Rove.

Page 53   "'Debbie Graves had . . .'" McRae, Moeller, Oliver interviews.

Page 53   "On the same day that . . ." Trial documents, McRae interview *Amarillo Daily News, Austin American-Statesman, Dallas Morning News* (January 24, 1990).

Page 53   "Rampton informed numerous . . ." Oliver interview, anonymous Agriculture Department sources.

Page 54   "The *Dallas Morning News* Austin bureau . . ." *Dallas Morning News* (February 14, 1990).

Page 54   "'The problems at TDA . . .'" *Houston Post* (June 27, 1990).

Page 54   "'I am the one who called in . . .'" Moeller interview.

Page 54   "Thursday morning's paper . . ." *Austin American-Statesman* (February 15, 1990).

Page 55   "According to Moeller, . . ." Moeller interview.

Page 55   "Vernie R. Glasson, executive . . ." Copy of Glasson letter (February 7, 1990).

Page 56   "According to numerous agriculture department workers . . ." Moeller, McRae, Oliver, anonymous Agriculture Department source interview.

Page 56   "'There are a lot of . . .'" Byron Sage, FBI agent interview.

Page 56   "'That's like saying . . .'" *Houston Post* (September 28, 1990).

Page 57   "'Let me think . . .'" *Texas Observer* (August 25, 2000).

Page 57   "'Nixonian dirty tricks' . . ." *Austin American-Statesman* (September 28, 1990).

Page 58   "'He did everything . . .'" Rick Perry interview (September 2002).

Page 58   "'I'm one hundred percent . . .'" McRae interview.

Page 58   "The man he named . . ." *Austin American-Statesman* (August 17, 1991).

Page 59   "'This begins to appear . . .'" *Austin American-Statesman* (August 17, 1991).

Page 59   "The closest Karl Rove . . ." *Houston Post* (June 27, 1990).

Page 60   "Spence was defending . . ." *Idaho Statesman* (May 26, 1993).

Page 60   "The shell came from . . ." *Idaho Statesman* (May 26, 1993).

Page 61   "You knew before the trial . . ." *New York Times* (May 28, 1993).

Page 61   "One of Rampton's colleagues . . ." *New York Times* (May 28, 1993).

Page 61   "'That's a bunch of crap . . .'" Byron Sage interview.

Page 62   "'These are phony . . .'" *Idaho Statesman* (May 26, 1990).

Page 62   "'I think that there's . . .'" *America Newsnet*, conservative radio network interview (November 23, 1999).

Chapter 6: Proof of Performance

Page 64   "'Logan,' he announced . . ." author Slater present.

Page 65   "'This was a big moment . . .'" author Slater present.

Page 67   "'Bush is the kind . . .'" *Dallas Observer* (May 13, 1999).

Chapter 7: The Boy Who Forgot to Be a Boy

Page 70   "Classmate Rick Higgins . . ." Author interview with Higgins (June 2002).

Page 70   "'He was so . . .'" Author interview with Hargreaves (June 2002).

Page 70   "'He was task-oriented . . .'" Author interview with Higgins (June 2002).

Page 71   "Sorenson, Rove's opponent . . ." Author interview with Sorenson (June 2002).

Page 71   "He quoted Napoleon: . . ." Rove campaign memo, Governor Bill Clements papers, Texas A&M University (September 1985).

Page 71   "Suddenly, into the gymnasium . . ." Rove campaign memo, Governor Bill Clements papers, Texas A&M University (September 1985); author interview with Rove (August 2002).

Page 72   "When he was . . ." *New York Times Magazine* (May 14, 2000).

Page 72   "His sister, Reba . . ." *Dallas Observer* (May 13, 1999).

Page 72   "Growing up . . ." Author interview with Rove (August 2002).

Page 73   "The star of . . ." Author interview with student Susan Galprin (June 2002).

Page 73   "'I didn't think . . .'" Author interview with Roark (June 2002).

Page 74   "The thing was . . ." Author interview with Langeland (July 2002).

Page 75   "'What would happen is . . .'" Author interview with Jones (July 2002).

Page 75   "One was the . . ." Author interview with Jones (July 2002).

Page 75   "Fellow student Eric . . ." Author interview with Kriesler (June 2002).

Page 75   "Once, Rove put . . ." Author interview with Langeland (July 2002).

Page 76   "'We were all . . .'" Author interview with Higgins (June 2002).

Page 76   "He and classmate . . ." Author interview with Gustavson (June 2002).

Page 77   "There is a . . ." *Odyssey 1969* Olympus High School year-book (May 1969).

Page 77   "Eldon Tolman's history . . ." Author interview with Gus-tavson (June 2002).

Page 78   "He ran errands . . ." *Salt Lake Tribune* (July 31, 2000).

Page 78   "'Karl was down . . .'" Author interview with Ludlow (July 2002).

Page 78   "At school, Rove . . ." Author interview with Gustavson (June 2002).

Page 79   "'He annoyed a . . .'"author interview with Gustavson (June 2002).

Page 79   "'Karl was a . . .'" Author interview with Smart (June 2002).

Page 79   "The first time . . ." Author interview with Rove (August 2002).

Page 79   "And here came . . ." Author interview with Gustavson (June 2002).

Page 79   "Tolman wanted his . . ." Author interview with Gustavson (June 2002).

Page 81   "'I always viewed . . .'" Author interview with Jones (July 2002).

Page 81   "Friend Mark Dangerfield . . ." *New York Times Magazine* (May 14, 2000).

Page 81   "His father, Louis . . ." Author interview with Rove (August 2002).

Page 82   "When Keith Roark . . ." Author interview with Roark (June 2002).

Page 82   "As a freshman . . ." Author interview with J. D. Williams (June 2002).

Page 83   "Rove never got . . ." Author interview with Rove.

Page 83   "'It was at the . . .'" Author interview with Bob Kjellander (June 2002).

Page 83   "He assumed a . . ." *Washington Post* (August 13, 1973).

Page 84   "'It was funny," Author interview with Kjellander (June 2002).

Page 84   "Dixon had a . . ." Author interview with Dixon (August 2002).

Page 84   "Rove rose swiftly . . ." application for Clements transition office, January 12, 1979, Governor Bill Clements papers, Texas A&M University.

Page 84   "At a seminar . . ." *Washington Post* (August 13, 1973).

Page 85   "'So one of . . .'" *Washington Post* (August 13, 1973).

Page 86   "In March, Rove . . ." author Slater interview with Rove (July 1994).

Page 86   "'I introduced Lee . . .'" author Slater interview with Rove (July 1994).

Page 87   "And in the end . . ." Author interview with Robert Edgeworth (July 2002).

Page 87   "It was a . . ." Author interview with Robert Edgeworth (July 2002).

Page 88   "The *Washington Post* . . ." *Washington Post* (August 13, 1973).

Page 89   "'He sent me . . .'" Author interview with Edgeworth (July 2002).

Page 89   "A few months . . ." author Slater interview with Rove (July 1994).

Chapter 8: Gone to Texas

Page 92   "'He was . . . cool' . . ." Author interview with Rove (March 1999).

Page 92   "'I was supposed . . .'" Rove deposition in 1996 tobacco lawsuit.

Page 92   "'We're not alike . . .'" Author interview with Rove (August 2002).

Page 92   "'Lee had a . . .'" Author interview with McBride (July 2002).

Page 93   "At dinner one . . ." Author interview with Rove associate.

Page 93   "But by then . . ." Author interview with Rove (August 2002).

Page 93   "The Virginia Republican . . ." *Austin Business Journal* (September 2, 1985).

Page 93   "As it turned . . ." Application for Clements transition office, January 12, 1979, Governor Bill Clements papers, Texas A&M University.

Page 95   "The elder Bush . . ." *Washington Post* (September 15, 1978).

Page 95   "Although paid from . . ." Rove deposition in tobacco lawsuit (1996).

Page 95   "'I am very . . .'" *Dallas Morning News* (June 2, 1978).

Page 95   "Reese offered a . . ." *Dallas Morning News* (June 2, 1978).

Page 96   "In 1979, Valerie . . ." Harris County divorce records.

Page 96   "'Okay, here are . . .'" Author interview with Rove (August 2002).

Page 97   "So Rove sat . . ." Rove campaign memo, Governor Bill Clements papers, Texas A&M University (September 1985).

Page 98   "'The whole art . . .'" Rove campaign memo, Governor Bill Clements papers, Texas A&M University (September 1985).

Page 98   "His job was . . ." Governor Bill Clements papers, Texas A&M University.

Page 99   "'It was a . . .'" Author interview with anonymous Republican colleague.

Page 99   "'Anti-White messages . . .'" Rove campaign memo, Governor Bill Clements papers, Texas A&M University (September 1985).

Page 99   "'That sort of . . .'" Author interview with Whittington (August 2002).

Page 100   "When a Houston . . ." Author interview with Wayne (August 2002).

Page 100   "At a reception . . ." *Dallas Morning News* (January 20, 1989).

Page 101   "The White House . . ." *Associated Press* (April 28, 1989).

Page 101   "'He got Lee . . .'" Author interview with Perry (July 2002).

Chapter 9: Refining the Crude

Page 104   "'Mr. Rove . . .'" Transcript of Senate Nominations Committee hearing (March 26, 1991).

Page 105   "'I was going . . .'" Author interview with Rove (August 2002).

Page 106 "His teaching partner . . ." Author interview with McNeely (June 2002).

Page 106 "'That's 1896 . . .'" Rove presentation.

Page 106 "When asked in . . ." Rove deposition in tobacco lawsuit (1996).

Page 106 "'He'd always wait . . .'" Author interview with Johnson (January 2000).

Page 107 "His college transcripts . . ." *The New Yorker* (November 8, 1999).

Page 107 "'I wasn't exactly . . .'" *Texas Monthly* (May 1994).

Page 107 "'The irony is . . .'" Author interview with Rove (August 2002).

Page 108 "'You know . . .'" *Midland Reporter-Telegram* (July 4, 1989).

Page 108 "In early 1993 . . ." Author interview with Toomey (January 2000).

Page 109 "'He didn't know . . .'" Author interview with Ratliff (August 2002).

Page 110 "'You sent me . . .'" Author interview with Wayne (August 2002).

Page 111 "Not so, said . . ." Author interview with Wayne (August 2002).

Page 111 "He was right . . ." Bush campaign finance reports filed with the Texas Ethics Commission.

Page 112 "'He would go . . .'" Author interview with Bush aide.

Page 112 "'I was never . . .'" George H. W. Bush, Doug Wead, *Man of Integrity* (Eugene, OR: Harvest House, 1988).

Page 112 "Once, when a friend . . ." Author interview with Bob Thomas (September 2002).

Page 113 "'In addition to . . .'" *National Review* (December 21, 1998).

Page 113 "A reporter from . . ." author Slater present.

Page 114 "'He was shaky . . .'" Author interview with Bush associate.

Page 114 "'Look, you are the . . .'" Author interview with Bush aide.

Page 114 "At campaign headquarters . . ." Bush campaign news releases.

Chapter 10: To the Victor

Page 115   "He was one . . ." *Forbes* (October 8, 2001).

Page 116   "'I want the . . .'" *Dallas Morning News* (December 4, 1990).

Page 116   "'Forget about environmental . . .'" *Dallas Morning News* (September 1, 1991).

Page 117   "'I have very . . .'" *Dallas Morning News* (September 1, 1991).

Page 118   "'We needed to . . .'" *Dallas Morning News* (September 19, 1992).

Page 118   "Rove picked up the . . ." author present.

Page 118   "'Nobody's going to . . .'" Author interview with McDonald (August 2002).

Page 119   "'I have one . . .'" Author interview with Williamson (August 2002).

Page 120   "At the State-Federal . . ." *Austin American-Statesman* (May 21, 1994).

Page 121   "'Do you have . . .'" Rove testimony in Travis County District Court, pretrial hearing (December 22, 1993).

Page 121   "Rove testified that . . ." author Slater present.

Page 121   "Not true . . ." Author interview with Elliott (June 2002).

Page 121   "'They mounted a . . .'" Author interview with Earl (November 2002).

Page 122   "In a political . . ." Texas Republican party news release.

Page 122   "His political investigators . . ." author present.

Page 122   "'The fact that . . .'" Author interview with Bonner (August 2002).

Page 122   "'I do my . . .'" Author interview with Miller (August 2002).

Page 124   "'For a while . . .'" Author interview with anonymous Republican colleague.

Page 124   "'There's something wrong . . .'" Author interview with anonymous Republican colleague.

Page 124   "'I'm going to . . .'" Author interview with anonymous Republican colleague.

Chapter 11: Contests without Rules

Page 125   "'I will be . . .'" *United Press International* (June 5, 1993).

Page 126   "'Hey, buddy . . .'" Author interview with Berry (November 2002).

Page 127   "'He looked at . . .'" Author interview with Sipple (August 2002).

Page 127   "Barbara Bush . . ." interview with Bush aide.

Page 128   "'They like her . . .'" *Dallas Morning News* (July 26, 1993).

Page 128   "It had Richards . . ." *The Texas Poll* (October 1993).

Page 129   "'He knew what . . .'" Author interview with Berry (November 2002).

Page 129   "His foray into . . ." *Houston Chronicle* (May 8, 1994).

Page 130   "'I like selling . . .'" *Time* (July 31, 1989).

Page 130   "He didn't even . . ." *Dallas Morning News* (May 2, 1989).

Page 130   "In promoting Bush . . ." *Dallas Morning News* (February 24, 1989).

Page 130   "'Am I going . . .'" author Slater interview with Bush (April 1994).

Page 131   "Bush turned and . . ." author Slater present.

Page 131   "'The sense was . . .'" Author interview with Rove (August 2002).

Page 131   "Rove suggested he . . ." Marvin Olasky, *The Tragedy of American Compassion* (Washington, DC: Regnery Gateway, 1992).

Page 132   "'The two issues . . .'" Marvin Olasky, *The Tragedy of American Compassion* (Washington, DC: Regnery Gateway, 1992).

Page 133   "'Limit GWB's public . . .'" Rove internal campaign memo.

Page 133   "'When you're developing . . .'" Author interview with Berry (November 2002).

Page 133   "'Bush puts down . . .'" Author interview with Berry (November 2002).

Page 133   "When Bush fumbled . . ." *Dallas Observer* (May 13, 1999).

Page 133   "'Is the Rove . . .'" author present.

Page 134   "Sipple produced virtually . . ." Ad texts, ad tape recordings.

Page 135   "'Crime is crime . . .'" Author interview with Sipple (August 2002).

Page 135   "'Here's what I'll . . .'" Author interview with Berry (November 2002).

Page 135   "'We can put . . .'" Author interview with Sipple (August 2002).

Page 136   "'You just work . . .'" *Houston Chronicle* (August 17, 1994).

Page 137   "'You have been . . .'" author Slater interview with Richards (August 1994).

Page 137   "Rove knew that . . ." Author interview with Republican colleague.

Page 137   "Bush set the . . ." Bush interview with Sam Attlesey (November 1993).

Page 138   "'There was clearly . . .'" Author interview with McDonald (August 2002).

Page 138   "Bush's East Texas . . ." *Houston Post* (August 26, 1994).

Page 139   "'This guy is . . .'" Author interview with Sipple (August 2002).

Chapter 12: Product Launch

Page 141   "'The politics of . . .'" Author interview with Rove (August 2002).

Page 142   "In Bush's first . . ." Bruce Buchanan interview with author.

Page 143   "Once, when a . . ." author Slater present.

Page 143   "Unlike the others . . ." Texas Ethics Commission finance reports.

Page 143   "'Our job is . . .'" Rove deposition in tobacco lawsuit (1996).

Page 144   "Periodically, Bush would . . ." *Boston Globe* (June 21, 1995).

Page 144   "'No one will . . .'" Author interview with anonymous Bush aide.

Page 144   "'Thank you . . .'" Author interview with anonymous Bush aide.

Page 145   "'You son of . . .'" Author interview with Pauken (June 2002).

Page 146   "'You have to . . .'" Author interview with Pauken (June 2002).

Page 146   "'Somewhere between . . .'" Author interview with Sadler (September 2002).

Page 146   "'I'd go down . . .'" Author interview with Rugeley (July 2002).

Page 147   "'I started getting . . .'" Author interview with Sadler (September 2002).

Page 147   "'I have absolutely . . .'" Author interview with Sadler (September 2002).

Page 148   "'What do you . . .'" Author interview with Sadler (September 2002).

Page 148   "'They've never been . . .'" Author interview with Sadler (September 2002).

Page 149   "'Where did this . . .'" Author interview with Sadler (September 2002).

Page 150   "'I'm ready . . .'" author present.

Page 150   "'They were long . . .'" Author interview with Berry (November 2002).

Chapter 13: Everything Matters

Page 151   "'Look here!' he said . . ." author Slater present.

Page 152   "'This was his . . .'" Author interview with McKinnon, first published in *American Journalism Review* (April 2001).

Page 153   "'Matthews,' Bush said . . ." author Slater present.

Page 154   "'If you are . . .'" Rove speech in Austin (November 12, 1999).

Page 155   "'He looked over . . .'" Author interview with Hughes (December 1999).

Page 155   "Rove held firm . . ." author Slater present.

Page 155   "While Bush toured . . ." author Slater present.

Page 156   "'Consultants don't concede . . .'" interviews with campaign aides.

Page 157   "'Thanks for calling . . .'" interviews with campaign aides.

Page 157   "'Karl was really . . .'" interview with anonymous Republican colleague.

Page 158   "Colyandro called it . . ." Author interview with Colyandro (July 2002).

Page 158   "The column said . . ." *Chicago Sun-Times* (September 18, 1992).

Page 159   "After the column . . ." Texas GOP Victory, 1992 release (September 18, 1992).

Page 159   "'The thing that . . .'" Author interview with Colyandro (July 2002).

Page 159   "In everything Rove . . ." *New York Times Magazine* (May 14, 2000).

Page 160   "'One day . . .'" author Moore interview with Neely (August 2002).

Page 162   "'What the hell . . .'" *Time* (February 14, 2000).

Page 162   "Rove didn't have . . ." Author interview with Rove (February 2000).

Page 163   "A professor from . . ." CNN *Inside Politics* (February 14, 2000).

Page 163   "'Don't give me . . .'" *Time* (March 21, 2000).

Page 163   "'People in this . . .'" interview with Karl Rove (February 19, 2000).

Chapter 14: Whose Dream Is This, Anyway?

Page 165   "It was 5 A.M. . . ," Author interview with Bush security officer (October 2000).

Page 167   "Stashed in one . . ." author Slater present.

Page 167   "'In 1980, it's . . .'" author Slater interview with Rove (June 2000).

Page 167   "'It's all visuals . . .'" author Slater present.

Page 167   "George W. has . . ." Author interview with Thurber (July 2000).

Page 169   "Rove, who was . . ." Author interview with Perry campaign aide (September 2002).

Page 169   "'I've won,' said . . ." author Slater present.

Page 170   "'People wanted to . . .'" Author interview with McKinnon (August 2000).

Page 170   "'I'm the first . . .'" author Slater present.

Page 173   "'It's become clear . . .'" author Slater present.

Page 173   "'I'm out!' he . . ." author Slater present.

Page 174   "As the year . . ." *New York Times* (December 2002).

Page 175   "Back home in . . ." Author interview with Weeks (August 2002).

Chapter 15: Rovian Cancer

Page 178   "'Iraq has developed . . .'" Author interview with Rove.

Page 178   "'Here's a guy . . .'" Author interview with Rove.

Page 179   "The plan was already being rolled . . ." The White House, National Security Strategy document, WhiteHouse.gov (September 17, 2002).

Page 179   "George W. Bush frequently told . . ." Bush stump speech, campaign 2002, author present, various.

Page 180   "'What if we haven't . . .'" anonymous Democratic source interview.

Page 181   "And this approach melded . . ." *Atlanta Constitution-Journal* (October 6, 2002).

Page 181   "'It was just brilliant . . .'" interview with author Moore.

Page 182   "Even the Central . . ." Letter of CIA Director George Tenet delivered to Congress, quoted by the *Associated Press* (September 28, 2002).

Page 182   "'I will not stand by . . .'" Text of president's speech, at WhiteHouse.gov.

Page 183   "'All of a sudden . . .'" anonymous Democrat interview.

Page 183   "Jim Jordan, the director . . ." *The New Republic* (September 23, 2002).

Page 184   "Card indicated the White House . . ." *New York Times* (September 7, 2002).

Page 185   "'The greater the threat . . .'" Text of president's speech, WhiteHouse.gov (September 20, 2002).

Page 185   "The president filled his . . ." CNN.com (September 9, 2002).

Page 186   "'The American example . . .'" *American Conservative* (October 21, 2002).

Page 186   "When he suggested . . ." *Arizona Republic* (September 26, 2002).

Page 187   "'So, I thought about . . .'" Author interview with Rove (Austin).

Page 187   "'Checking a box . . .'" Buchanan interview, University of Texas.

Page 188   "According to the . . ." *Washington Post* article quoted in *American Conservative* (November 18, 2002).

Page 188   "But the White House kept . . ." *American Conservative* (December 2, 2002).

Page 189   "'It is almost eerie . . .'" anonymous political analyst interview.

Index

A

Agriculture department,
    investigation of, 45–46
Allbaugh, Joe, 142, 174
Alwin, Larry, 44, 50
American Enterprise Institute, 7
Arbusto Energy, 129
Armey, Dick, 119
Ashcroft, John, 126
Attlesey, Sam, 21, 23, 30, 211
Atwater, Lee, 14, 21, 30, 31, 85,
    92, 101, 162
  compared to Rove, 92
Auditor's report, 51
Aziz, Tareq, 189

B

Baker, James A. III, 94
Bashur, Reggie, 21, 26
Bayoud, George, 19, 21, 30, 32
Beauchamp, Larry, 5, 39, 40, 41,
    42, 58, 200
Begala, Paul, 106
Bennett, Wallace, 78, 80

Berry, Brian, 126, 142, 150
Betts, Roland, 107
Board of International
    Broadcasting, 49, 57
Bob Jones University, 164
Bonner, Cathy, 119, 122
Boyd, Bob, 45, 52, 53, 55, 58
Bruni, Frank, 64
Bryan, William Jennings, 7
Buchanan, Bruce, 1, 142, 187,
    197, 211
Bugging incident, 17–26
  FBI reports, 31–33
  film about, 34, 36
  fraudulent incident, 5
  questions about, 27–37
Building Texas Agriculture,
    45–46, 54
Bullock, Bob, 57, 105, 142
Burston-Wade, Deborah, 142
Bush, Barbara, 127
Bush, George H. W., 49, 86
  Republican National
    Committee chairman, 86
Bush, George W.:
  Air National Guard, 91
  arrest, 170

campaign for governor,
110–114, 126–139
campaign in New Hampshire,
151–164
and crime, 134
and education, 134
educational policy, 113
free market philosophy, 4
as governor, 9–12
Harvard, 91, 106
losing, 158
National Guard, 91, 186
power, 2
presidential campaign, 142
on property taxes, 141–146
relationship with Rove, 1–2,
6, 123
Texas Rangers, 102, 129–130
2000 election, 4
Bush Exploration, 129
Business taxes, 141

C

Carbaugh, John, 86
Card, Andy, 184
Carney, James, 2
Castro, Fidel, 178
Cheney, Dick, 181, 191, 193
Chicago Boys, 87
Childs, Diana, 77
Christian, George, 98
Christian Coalition, 163

Citizens for the Republic, 94
Clear Skies Initiative, 17
Cleland, Max, 186
Clements, Bill, 5, 18–19, 22, 25,
41–42, 96–98, 104,
146–147, 157, 167
Clements, Jaime, 19, 28
Clinton, Bill, 128
Clinton, William, 103
College Republican National
Committee, 86
College Republicans, 82–88
Colyandro, John, 158
Consultants' role, 6–8
Cooper, Matt, vi
Corruption, claims of, 42–43
Cox, John, 115–116
Credit card use, 39–40

D

Dallas Cowboys, 112
Dangerfield, Mark, 81
Daschle, Tom, 180
Datt, John C., 55
Davis, Tommy, 33
Debate, Clements/White, 25–26
Deguerin, Dick, 121
Diamond, Harris, 21, 30–32
Direct mail, Clements'
campaign, 98
Direct-mail business, 93, 98,
143

Dirty tricks, 6
Dixon, Alan, 83
Dole, Bob, 145
Dowd, Maureen, 152

E

Earle, Ronnie, 120, 121
East Texas State University,
    104
Edgar, Jim, 134
Edgeworth, Robert, 87
Elliot, David, 40, 45, 121
Enron, 111, 132, 146
Evans, Don, 3, 167

F

Fair, Mike, 162
FBI, 20, 21
Fitzgerald, Patrick, vi, 191
Francis, Jim, 158
Free market philosophy, 4
Front porch campaign, 154
Fund for Limited Government,
    94

G

Garcia, Guillermo X., 29
Gay marriage issues, 189

Geneva Convention, comments
    about, 172
Glasgow, Bob, 47, 104
Glasson, Vernie R., 55
Global warming, 17
Goobergate, 27
Governor's Business Council, 111
Gramm, Phil, 42, 125, 159
Graves, Debbie, 47, 53–54
Gregg, Judd, 151
Gubernatorial debate, 5
Guerrero, Lena, 116–119
Gustavson, Mark, 75, 76

H

Halliburton, 195
Hammond, Reba, 72
Hance, Kent, 95
Hanna, Mark, 7, 154
Hargreaves, Glenn, 70
Hatch, Orrin, 102
Healthy Forests Initiative, 17
Helms, Jesse, 86
Hickie, Jane, 119, 122
Higgins, Rick, 70, 76
Hightower, Jim, 5, 39–41, 44,
    46, 49, 51, 55, 61, 101, 105
    agriculture commisioner, 39
Hinckley, Bob, 82
Hinckley Institute, 82
Hoppe, Christy, 54
Hound Dog meter, 28

Hughes, Karen, 64, 122, 142,
    148, 170, 172, 193
Humphrey, Hubert, 76, 79, 80
Hutchison, Kay Bailey, 99, 101,
    119, 120, 125
  misuse of funds, 120

I

Inouye, Daniel, 186
Iowa, presidential campaign,
    12–13, 63
Iraq, 17–18, 76, 177–195
"Iron Triangle, The," 142, 174
Ivins, Molly, 57

J

Johnson, Clay, 106
Johnson, Glenn, 64
Johnson, Lyndon, 76, 80, 96,
    98, 109
Johnson, Paul, 113
Jong-il, Kim, 188
Jordan, Jim, 183

K

Karl Rove and company, 12, 19,
    20, 35
  bugging incident, 5, 26, 34
  investigation of, 27–37

Katrina, vi, vii
Keene, Judy, 64
Kerry, John, 127, 184
Kiesler, Eric, 75
Kjellander, Bob, 83
Knight Diversified Services, 18,
    27, 29, 33
Koontz, Russell, 45, 53, 58

L

LaMontagne, Margaret, 148
Langeland, Emil, 74
Lay, Ken, 111, 132
Lenz, Mary, 56
Lesbian/Gay Rights Lobby, 137
Logan, Dave, 29
Luce, Ken, 102
Ludlow, Randy, 78, 89
Lumet, Sidney, 34
Lyon, Matt, 25, 36

M

Magnet, Myron, 112
Matthews, Chris, 152
Mauro, Garry, 5, 43, 105,
McBride, Richard, 92
McCain, Cindy, 163
McCain, John, 13, 123, 127,
    139
McDonald, Chuck, 118, 138
McKinley, William, 7, 154

McKinnon, Mark, 26, 34, 152, 170
McRae, Pete, 6, 42, 44, 46, 49, 50, 53, 58, 60, 190
"Meet the Press," 154, 155
Midland, Texas, 3
Mike the Knife, 109
Military draft, 76
Miller, Bill, 122
Mills, Dan, 44
Moeller, Mike, 6, 44, 45, 46, 49, 52, 54, 55, 58, 60, 190
Morphew, Gary L., 18
Mosbacher, Rob Jr., 158

N

National Rifle Association (NRA), 85, 93
National Security Strategy, 185
Neely, Joe, 159
New Hampshire, presidential campaign, 9, 12–15
Nixon, Richard, 72, 79
North American Free Trade Agreement (NAFTA), 4
North Korea, 178, 186–188
Novak, Robert, vi, 159

O

O'Brien, Larry, 85
Olasky, Marvin, 112, 131

Oliver, Jesse, 44, 50
Owen, Priscilla, 100

P

Parsing words, 103
Pelosi, Alexandra, 156
Pennsylvania, in 2000 election, 4
Permanent consultant, 7
Perot, Ross, 107
Perry, Bob, 132
Perry, Rick, 5, 40, 41, 42, 47, 51, 52–54, 58, 99, 101, 168
    campaign for agriculture commissioner, 40–42
    governor's race, 58
Petroleum Club, 94
Philip Morris, 132
Phillips, Tom, 99, 110
Pilgrim, Lonnie "Bo," 132
Plame, Valerie, vi, 18, 24, 103, 159, 190, 192, 193
Political action committee (PAC), 45, 46, 54
Political consultant, Rove's philosophy, 103
Political consulting, 19, 34
    movie about, 34–35
Political strategies, 2, 3
Politics at the White House, 2
Powell, Colin, 3
Power, 34, 35

Presidential campaign:
  New Hampshire debate,
    9–10, 12
Presidential primary, mistakes,
  10–13
Property taxes, 141
Public Integrity Unit of Travis
  County, 39, 41
Pyongyang, 188

Q

Quicksall, Bill, 58

R

Rampton, Calvin, 78, 80
Rampton, Greg, 5, 20, 43, 48,
  49, 52, 56, 57, 59, 60, 62,
  104
  in Idaho, 60–61
  improper use of authority,
    56
  and Randy Weaver, 60–62
  transfer out of Austin, 61
Ratliff, Bill, 109, 138
Reagan, Ronald, 97, 167
Real Plans for Real People, 170
Reed, Ralph, 163
Reese, Jim, 94
Reformer With Results, 162
Republican National Committee,
  66, 84, 86, 89, 92, 93

Richards, Ann, 97, 101, 104,
  108, 110, 113, 114, 116,
  117, 119, 122, 123, 125,
  127, 128, 135, 137, 142
  campaign against Bush,
    113–114, 115–124
  1990 governor's race,
    127–128
Roark, Keith, 73, 82
Robinson, Bernie, 84
Rove, Karl, 58–61, 64–67,
  69–72, 77, 82–84, 89, 91,
  95–97, 100, 103–104,
  113–114, 117, 126, 138,
  142, 144–145, 151, 157,
  161, 164, 175, 179–181,
  183, 185–194
  advisor, redefined role, 6
  answering questionaire, 49–50
  College Republican National
    Committee, 86–88
  as compared to Atwater, 92
  credibility, 48
  on Cuba, 178
  debate club, 73–77
  direct mail, 96, 138, 143
  divorce from Valerie, 96
  first meeting with G. W.
    Bush, 81
  high school career, 69–89
  influence of, 1–2
  and Iraq, 177–178
  language, use of, 177
  and Lee Atwater, 85–87
  marriage to Valerie, 93

meeting with Rampton, 48–49
on property taxes, 141–150
reading habits, 112–113
relationship with Bush, 6
school years, 70–72
Vietnam war, 69
Rove, Reba Wood, 72
Rove, Valerie, divorce from
    Karl, 96
Ruby Ridge trial, 60
Rugeley, Cindy, 146
Russert, Tim, 154

S

Sadler, Paul, 146, 148
Sage, Byron, 21, 44, 56, 61
Salazar, Rossanna, 146
Sawyer–Miller Group, 31
Schieffer, Tom, 130
School tax plan (Texas), 145
Schroeder, Paul W., 186
Scott, Bruce Wayne, 18
Shaping policy, 2
Shapiro, Florence, 148
Sherman, Max, 105
Sipple, Don, 126
Slater, Wayne, 64–65
    confrontation with Rove, 64
Smart, Chris, 79
Smith, Glenn, 60
Smith, Ralph, 83
Smith, Tom, 59
Sorensen, John, 69

South Carolina, presidential
    campaign, 39
Spectrum, 129
Spence, Gerry, 60
Stanford, Jason, 181
Steel, tariffs on imports, 4
Stiles, Mark, 148
Stone, Black, Manafort and
    Atwater, 31
Straight Talk Express, 155
Subpoena, on Bob Boyd, 52
"Suddenly Saddam" strategy, 182
Superconducting Supercollider,
    36

T

Tariffs on imported steel, 4
Team Bush first victory, 64, 173
Texas:
    school tax plan, 145
    school vouchers, 149
Texas Air National Guard, 91,
    186
Texas Association of Business,
    110
Texas Chili Parlor, 101, 154
Texas Department of Agriculture
    (TDA), 46, 50, 53–56, 59
    audits of, 39
    federal investigation, 5, 41,
    57, 59
Texas Department of Public
    Safety (DPS), 20, 28, 33

Texas Farm Bureau, 55
Texas Federal Inspection Service,
    49
  contract with building Texas
      Agriculture, 45
  relatioinship with Texas
      Department of
      Agriculture, 5
Texasgate, 26
Texas Public Citizen, 59
Texas Railroad Commission, 116
Texas Rangers, 102, 107, 109,
    125, 129, 130
Thigpen, Joseph, 40
Thurber, James, 167
Tierney Alofsin, Patricia, 26, 36
Tomaso, Bruce, 42, 44
Toomey, Mike, 108
Travis county district attorney,
    5, 20, 39, 40

U

United Nations, 184
U.S. Department of Agriculture
    (USDA), 39–40, 42, 50,
    52, 55, 58
  audit of Texas-Federal, 40

V

Virginia Republican party, 93

W

Wall, Thomas, 42
Wallace, George, 79
Walters, Logan, 64, 165
War on terrorism and politics,
    180–181, 183–184, 187,
    194
Wayne, Ralph, 100, 109, 111
Wead, Doug, 112
Weapons of mass destruction
    (WMD), 18
Weaver, John, 36, 123
Weaver, Randy, 60, 61, 62
Weeks, David, 175
West Virginia, in 2000 election,
    4
White, Mark, 19, 21–22, 24–25,
    28, 31–36, 97, 99, 104
Whittington, Harry, 99
Williams, Clayton, 101
Williams, J. D., 82
Williamson, Barry, 117, 118
Wilson, Pete, 134
WMUR–TV, 9
Wolfowitz, Paul, 181
Wood, Buck, 43
Woodward, Bob, 139

Y

Young Americans for Freedom
    (YAF), 83

About the Authors

JAMES MOORE is an Emmy Award–winning TV news correspondent with more than a quarter century of print and broadcast experience. He has traveled extensively on every presidential campaign since 1976. His reports have appeared on CNN, NBC, and CBS. His professional honors include an Emmy from the National Academy of Television Arts and Sciences, the Edward R. Murrow Award from the Radio Television News Director's Association, and the Individual Broadcast Achievement Award from the Texas Headliners' Foundation.

WAYNE SLATER is the Bureau Chief of the Dallas Morning News in Austin, Texas. He has traveled extensively, covering national and state politics for the newspaper. Mr. Slater traveled full-time for eighteen months covering the presidential campaign of George W. Bush. He has covered every Republican and Democratic national convention since 1988, six sessions of the Texas Legislature, and the administrations of Texas Governors Bill Clements, Ann Richards, and George W. Bush. Mr. Slater is a frequent guest on numerous network and cable political programs.